Man, Mind and Land

A THEORY OF RESOURCE USE

Man, Mind and Land

A THEORY OF RESOURCE USE

234639

BY WALTER FIREY

GREENWOOD PRESS, PUBLISHERS
WESTPORT, CONNECTICUT

Library of Congress Cataloging in Publication Data

Firey, Walter Irving, 1916-
   Man, mind, and land.

   Reprint of the ed. published by the Free Press,
Glencoe, Ill.
   Bibliography: p.
   Includes index.
   1. Natural resources. I. Title.
[HC55.F5 1977]   333.7   77-12902
ISBN 0-8371-9834-8

Reprinted in 1977 by   Greenwood Press, Inc.
                     51 Riverside Avenue
                     Westport, CT. 06880

Printed in the United States of America

To Mary Lou

ACKNOWLEDGMENTS

THE STUDY on which this volume is based had its beginning in an inter-university seminar sponsored by the Social Science Research Council and held at Ann Arbor, Michigan during the summer of 1952. Financial assistance for an important part of the data-gathering and writing phases of the study was provided by the Research Institute of the University of Texas. Indispensable criticism of particular sections of the manuscript was offered by Dr. Murray E. Polakoff, Dr. Clyde L. Hardin and Dr. William J. Firey. The editors of *Human Organization* and *Rural Sociology* kindly granted permission to reproduce two articles which had previously appeared in their journals—specifically, Chapter VIII, which incorporates most of the paper "Coalition and Schism in a Regional Conservation Program," *Human Organization,* XV, No. 4 (1957), 17-20; and Chapter IX, which incorporates most of the paper "Patterns of Choice and the Conservation of Resources," *Rural Sociology,* XXII, No. 2 (1957), 113-22.

WALTER FIREY

Austin, Texas
March 21, 1959

CONTENTS

I	INTRODUCTION	11
II	APPROACHES TO NATURAL RESOURCES	19
III	DIFFERENCES AMONG RESOURCE OPTIMA	39
IV	THE RANGE AND LIMITS OF A RESOURCE COMPLEX	55
V	THE SOCIAL STATICS OF A RESOURCE COMPLEX	81
VI	THE SOCIAL DYNAMICS OF A RESOURCE COMPLEX	111
VII	THE DEVELOPMENT OF NATURAL RESOURCES	135
VIII	THE USE OF NATURAL RESOURCES	165
IX	THE CONSERVATION OF NATURAL RESOURCES	207
X	CONSENT AS A CONDITION OF RESOURCE PLANNING	243
	INDEX	253

CHAPTER I

INTRODUCTION

> The more the island of knowledge expands in the sea of ignorance, the larger its boundary to the unknown.
>
> L. S. RODBERG AND
> V. F WEISSKOPF [1]

MOST GOVERNMENTS TODAY are committed to the idea that they can improve their people's use of land and resources. In countries which are close to the subsistence level, the purpose is usually a fuller exploitation of those natural resources. In other countries, particularly the more industrialized ones, the goal is likely to be the conservation of natural resources. In either case, there is the intention of making some change in present uses of land and resources.

The idea that a government can change customary practices in the use of natural resources rests on some assumptions concerning the necessary and sufficient conditions for successful planning. There is no doubt that changes in resource practices do at times accompany deliberate efforts in that direction. It is just as true that such changes sometimes take place anyway, without governmental intervention. On still other occasions, customary resource practices prove to be quite resistant to governmental planning efforts. This ambiguity in the relationship between plans and results is an obvious deterrent to rational policy making. Without dependable knowledge of the conditions for successful planning, resource policies are likely to turn into rash adventures, opportunistic compromises or unaccountable triumphs and failures.

Of course some discrepancy between plans and results is inherent in all purposive behavior, individual as well as social. In the case of governmental planning, however, the political consequences of such a discrepancy are likely to confront the planner with an ideological problem: how is he to explain his miscalculation? What general principles can he invoke which would, as it were, account for his errors by stating some systematic connections between them and various other kinds of events? Putting the matter in another way, what general theory may there be which will specify the necessary and sufficient conditions for effecting changes in people's use of land and resources?

A starting point for developing such a theory is given in the observation that man's use of his natural resources has many of the properties of an organic whole. This is true in two respects: (1) Particular types of resource use seem to have unique patterns of their own. Thus hoe cultivation and plow cultivation represent distinctive systems of agriculture, each having characteristic field contours and crop rotations which maintain their respective patterns over widely scattered parts of the world. (2) There seem to be some patterns which characterize *all* resource systems, whatever their particular type. Depletion of an exhaustible resource, for instance, generally goes through some one of a limited number of sequences, involving thus a constriction on the logically possible number of sequences.

The existence of such patterns in resource phenomena is warrant for our establishing some conceptual distinctions. We may begin by considering natural resources as a type of landed capital, differing from other types of capital only in the relatively greater part which non-human *events* occupy in their development. For our purpose an *event* may be defined as a unique space-time coincidence of happenings, such as a moldboard plow turning a furrow slice at a particular instant of time. An event which recurs in time and which involves somewhat the same combination of human and biophysical factors may be called a *resource process*. Thus, plowing with oxen constitutes one process; plowing with horses constitutes another process. To the economist a process may be identified with a particular proportioning of some designated productive factors.[2] To the ecologist or geographer, a process may be identified with a particular association of organic and physical elements in a given habitat. Processes, then, represent the elemental units out of which natural resources are built. As components of landed capital, they contribute to the realization of a people's standards of living.

By way of further conceptual elaboration, we may adopt the term *resource system* as a generic designation of any set of resource processes, irrespective of the structural character which that set may or may not have. Thus, a particular resource system might be viewed as consisting of the tools which are customarily employed, the combinations and sequences in which they are used; the animals employed, their equipment, care, habits and seasonal characteristics; the crops grown, their growth patterns, soil tolerances, planting, cultivation and harvesting sequences; the soils cultivated, their structure, chemistry and micro-organismic activity; the productive organization of the population, its market forms, specialization of labor and land division; the relevant conceptual categories, empirical knowledge, and magical beliefs possessed by a people; and, finally, a particular nexus of organic and physical processes such as photosynthesis, symbiosis, evaporation, etc. In the present study, any such set of resource processes will be referred to as a *resource system*.

It is possible, now, to distinguish two varieties of resource systems according to the presence or absence of some determinate structure within a set of resource processes. Both varieties are to be taken as limiting cases. One of them, which we propose to call a *resource complex*, shows some constancy and stability in the face of changes that are external to itself. The other, which we shall call a *resource congeries*, shows no such stability but varies widely in response to external changes. The former type of system has a certain lawfulness which expresses the invariance properties that it possesses as a structural whole; its component processes may be given a special designation: *resource practices*. The other type of system is an indeterminate entity; its component processes require no special designation.[3]

Introduction

Throughout the course of this study we shall be primarily concerned with developing the implications of viewing resource phenomena in terms of their structural properties. If we can establish the proposition that the resource processes of a people do at times form a structural whole, and if we can further show that resource phenomena as a class exhibit some generic invariance properties, we shall have made some progress toward learning the necessary and sufficient conditions for successful resource planning. We shall have at least defined some outer bounds within which governments must operate in seeking to improve their people's use of land and resources.

A resource system, we are going to find, is a man-mind-land structure which imposes a special kind of constraint or necessity upon its human agents such that there is a sufficient reason for them to willingly conform their behavior to the practices which comprise that resource system. Of course, this constraint or necessity is rarely perceived in so formal a manner by the individual human agent who experiences it. For his part, the farmer, miner, or fisherman knows no such thing as a resource system, much as Molière's hero knew no such thing as prose. Yet in both instances the individual finds himself making his behavior comply with a limited range of practices which thereby take on a structure. The English villein in his thirteenth century open fields and the Texas irrigation cotton grower on his twentieth century factory farm, each has experienced his respective resource system as a phenomenal necessity, yet a necessity which he has accepted and, indeed, willed.

In the chapters which follow, we propose to describe and analyze four distinct resource systems, two of them belonging to folk societies, one belonging to a feudal society, and the other belonging to an industrial society.[4] This selection of cases has been designed to cover a wide gamut of geographical and technological variants. As such, it should offer a fairly broad perspective on man's use of land and resources under different physical and cultural regimes. It is hoped that the expository account of these four resource systems will be of some interest in its own right. More than this, though, our analysis of cases is intended to illustrate a type of cross-cultural analysis in which suitably generalized variables can be rendered as equivalent between cultures so that specific hypotheses, stated in terms of these variables, may be tested or illustrated. Above all, however, our interest lies in some particular empirical hypotheses about resource phenomena. These hypotheses purport to be universally true descriptions of the activities of human beings as resource users. They purport, too, to be so interrelated with one another as to form important components of a systematic theory of natural resources. The symbolism and the syntax in which they are stated may afford a more realistic approach to resource phenomena than that which has hitherto been available for resource analysis. To appreciate this possibility, let us first undertake a brief survey of the principal approaches which presently dominate the study of natural resources.

NOTES

1. L. S. Rodberg and V. F. Weisskopf, "Fall of Parity," *Science,* CXXV (1957), 632.
2. Or range of proportions.
3. The term "resource complex" has been suggested by J. R. Whitaker

in "Sequence and Equilibrium in Destruction and Conservation of Natural Resources," *Annals of the Association of American Geographers,* XXXI (1941), 129-44. The term "resource congeries" is a special case of the more general concept "congeries" developed by Pitirim A. Sorokin in *Social and Cultural Dynamics* (New York: American Book Co., 1937, 1941), vol. IV, chap. i, and in *Society, Culture and Personality* (New York: Harper and Bros., 1947), chap. xvii. For a formal logical analysis of the concept "complex" and other wholistic constructs, see: Nicholas Rescher and Paul Oppenheim, "Logical Analysis of Gestalt Concepts," *British Journal for the Philosophy of Science,* VI (1955), 89-106. My own application of these concepts has been heavily influenced by the approach (employing somewhat different terminology) developed in an article by P. de Schlippe and B. L. Batwell, "Preliminary Study of the Nyangwara System of Agriculture," *Africa,* XXV (1955), 321-51; cf. Pierre de Schlippe, *Shifting Cultivation in Africa* (London: Routledge and Kegan Paul Ltd., 1956).

4. On the rationale for this typology of societies see Gideon Sjoberg, "Folk and 'Feudal' Societies," *American Journal of Sociology,* LVIII (1952), 231-39.

CHAPTER II

APPROACHES TO NATURAL
RESOURCES

> . . . with a true view, all the data
> harmonize, but with a false one,
> the facts soon clash.
> ARISTOTLE *

$\mathcal{P}$LATO'S IDEAL of a government by philosopher kings could never work for reasons which lie in the very nature of a social order. So too, there are ideals of resource development and conservation which can never be built into any social order.

This baldly stated proposition, we submit, is bound up with the hypothesis that a resource system is an organic whole which comports with only a limited range of practices. A going resource system owes its character to more compelling forces than the ideals of individuals or the vagaries of governments. There are mechanisms operating in every social order that forever sift and sort the resource processes which are possible in a given habitat or which are conceivable in a given culture. The outcome of this "natural selection" is a resource system having invariance properties which are givens for any government that would seek to change its people's customs. In subsequent chapters, we shall describe some of these mechanisms of natural selection and shall try to discover why some resource processes enter into a resource system and why others do not.

At this point, however, it will be instructive to take a reconnaissance of the range of knowledge which pertains to natural resources. At least three broad groupings of such knowledge can be distinguished. Each of them is a category of descriptive information and each involves a distinct frame of reference for explaining resource phenomena. Each of them, too, yields a number of generalized propositions which can serve as canons for resource planning and policy formation. The first of them takes the physical habitat as its point of departure; the second starts with the culture of the human being; the third begins with the attribute of scarcity which attaches to human activities. These three approaches may be called, respectively, the ecological, the ethnological, and the economic, bearing in mind that in these terms we have rather arbitrary designations for bodies of knowledge which have been developed by a number of disciplines.[1] To each of them there corresponds a theory, or at least a proto-theory, which orders information around a few generalized and logically interrelated propositions about resource phenomena.

In the pages which follow, we are going to undertake a brief characterization of these three approaches. Our principal interest will lie in the generalized theoretical propositions which accompany each of them. Above all, we shall try to identify the particular resource processes which are construed as optimal by the theories or proto-theories in question. In the course of our reconnaissance, too, we shall attempt to disengage the formal arguments which are implicit in each of the three approaches. Finally, from the conclusions of these formal arguments, we shall derive a preliminary hypothesis concerning the mode of relationship which obtains between the data of the three groupings of resource knowledge: the ecological, the ethnological, and the economic.

The ecological approach to resource phenomena has been developed mainly by botanists, zoologists, and geographers. The basic referential category in this approach may be variously designated as *equilibrium, stability,* or *balance.* These are terms which depict a state of nature in which the plants, animals, and physical features of a habitat are so interrelated as to form an *ecosystem*—an entity whose chemical elements circulate along regular paths between organisms and the environment. In every ecosystem there exists a more or less self-regulating *biotic community* comprised of its own characteristic association (or range of associations) of species whose survival is only possible in such a community. Not all features of a people's culture may conform to this state of nature; hence, elements of the latter comprise only a proper subset of the former. Expressed as the major premise in a syllogism, the assumption is that a set of resource processes, if it is to be "possible" in a given habitat,[2] must be in some degree of equilibrium with that habitat. The minor premise asserts that there are resource complexes which would not be in equilibrium with some habitats. The conclusion which follows is that there are resource complexes which would not be possible in some habitats. I.e.:

Every set of resource processes which is possible for a given organic and physical environment is one which would be in equilibrium with that environment.

There is at least one set of resource processes existing somewhere as a resource complex which would not be in equilibrium with a given organic and physical environment.

Therefore there is at least one set of resource processes existing somewhere as a resource complex which, for a given organic and physical environment, is not a possible set of resource processes.

This conclusion yields an important class of resource processes, viz., those which would not be possible in a given organic and physical environment. In this reasoning, there can be only brief interludes during which man's resource processes may exceed the inexorable limits that are imposed by nature. As an "ecologic dominant" over much of the earth man is,[3] to be sure, capable of upsetting the balance comprised of soil structure, water movements, microorganismic activity, and plant and animal nutrition—but only at the cost of his long run well being.

A good deal of supportive evidence may be adduced on behalf of both premises in this argument. Consider the first of them. Plants are known to have definite limits in their adaptive capacities, some having greater tolerance for negative factors in the environment than others, but all having minimal requirements in respect to carbon, hydrogen, oxygen, temperature, and mineral nutrients, as well as to the proportions and sequences in these factors. Animals, too, as links in a food chain, have minimal requirements in respect to calories, proteins, calcium, salt, iron, vitamins, and innumerable trace elements. Insufficiency in any of these nutritional elements will lead to plant and animal diseases and to impaired survival capacity for the species concerned.

Given, then, a particular habitat, with its soil structure, its terrain, and its climate, there is only a limited range of plant and animal associations which can be possibly sustained. Resource practices which require or give rise to plant and animal associations exceeding this limited range will not last. Thus, the critical depletion of certain mineral elements in the soil by single cropping, or a disturbance in the balance of plant and animal species by introduction of alien species can destroy the food chain of which man is a member. Improper irrigation will lead to salinization and hence to barrenness of the soil. The plowing of tropical lands or of grasslands will damage their granular structure and with it their capacity to absorb and hold water. Such practices as these are self destructive. By disrupting a natural equilibrium, they impair the life carrying capacity of the land and lead, by any of several possible routes, to their own extinction.

The first premise, then, may be taken as a real (and not a nominal) definition of the set of resource processes which will be possible in any given habitat. In regard to the minor premise of the argument, there are many well documented accounts of resource complexes which, by even the loosest criteria, could not have been in equilibrium with their own or other organic and physical environments. Nomadic goat herding in the Mediterranean region affords one of the more spectacular examples of an unbalanced resource complex. Deteriorated soils and eroded lands resulting from overgrazing by close cropping goats bear witness to a faulty man-land relationship throughout much of Spain, Italy, Greece, Libya, and Algeria. Wheat growing in the semi-arid Great Plains of North America, slash-and-burn agriculture in the North Andean highlands, and plow agriculture in tropical Africa are further examples of resource complexes which are not in equilibrium with organic and physical processes.

From the foregoing premises, it follows that there are resource complexes which would not be possible for some habitats. When this conclusion is coupled with the normative proposition that certain valued practices within a particular resource complex ought nevertheless to be proselyted (e.g., plowing), the inference can be drawn that a change in other elements of that complex may have to be accomplished. In any such change, the object would be to establish a reconstituted resource complex which, while retaining the valued elements of the original complex, will now be in equilibrium with certain specified habitats.

One criterion for determining which subset of resource processes, within the larger set of possible resource processes, will best comport with a natural equilibrium is the concept of *climax*. Climax is a hypothetical final stage to which the successive biotic communities of a habitat are assumed to tend, a stage at which there is such an association of plants and animals as can perpetuate itself in that habitat throughout the course of a given climatic regime. Human intervention in the natural trend of organic and physical processes is conceived as fixing the biotic community at some stage below climax. Since, of course, the agency of man is a rather ubiquitous feature of the earth's landscape, a modification of the concept has been proposed by Tansley. He suggests the term *anthropogenic climax,* having in mind the particular stabilization of plant and animal associations that ensues from a consistent and prolonged type of land use by man.[4] Thus, particular field forms, such as hedges, will give rise to characteristic communities of birds, insects, and grasses which are predicated on the maintenance of those field forms by man. Anthropogenic climax may be viewed as that particular association of plants and animals which is able to perpetuate itself in a habitat throughout the course of a given type of human occupancy.

Anthropogenic climax thus defines a subset of optimum resource processes within the more inclusive set of possible resource processes. It is this subset which is "best," given the normative proposition that the maintenance or extension of certain resource processes is desirable and given the premise that equilibrium with the environment is a necessary condition for such maintenance or extension.

This, then, would seem to be the subset which should serve as the goal for resource planning and policy making. Attaining such an optimum resource complex would, of course, entail far-reaching changes in most social orders. It is too much to expect that human agents will freely abandon present resource practices and adopt new ones for the sake of an abstract goal such as this. Some more compelling reason must be given a population to induce it to accept a change in its resource practices, even when that change will achieve anthropogenic climax.

At this point, of course, the argument has carried us into another frame of reference. From premises of an ecological order we have moved to premises concerning the social order. The idea that human agents *can* be motivated to make their behavior comply with a subset of optimum resource practices rests on sociological and psychological assumptions. It supposes that the social order, comprised as it is of human activities in their interpersonal aspect, can be freely remade after the image of an ideal. It assumes that the processes which are optimal by ecological criteria are likewise viable by ethnological, economic, or other criteria, such that there will be voluntary conformity to them by human agents. The difficulties which are bound up with this assumption have been aptly pointed out by Furon, who writes:

It is clear, therefore, that any immediate and drastic introduction of the measures proper for soil conservation would lead to revolution or to widespread discontent. To minimize these extreme and unnecessary effects, it will be necessary to undertake a skillful propaganda program. Such propaganda will be skillful to the extent that it takes account of the psychological reactions of those to whom it is addressed.[5]

We are led thus to the two approaches which are most relevant to an understanding of the "psychological reactions" of human agents as resource users. These are the ethnological and the economic approaches to natural resources. We may consider them in that order.

The ethnological approach to resource phenomena has been developed principally by anthropologists and sociologists, though to a lesser extent by geographers and ecologists as well. Indeed, there is an interesting correspondence between the two bodies of theory. Ecologists since Uexküll have emphasized the selective nature of an organism's reaction to its environment, whereby different species may have altogether different *ambients* though they all occupy the same habitat. So, too, ethnologists have established the fact that, as Spoehr puts it, ". . . different peoples inhabiting the same or very similar habitats . . . have made use of different sectors of the resources of their habitat." [6] The explanation for this selectivity lies in the cultural unlikeness of different peoples.

The culture of a people consists of a set of *activities,* including a language with its vocabulary and syntax and a fund of beliefs and techniques for classifying, evaluating, and manipulating phenomena. In any culture there is usually a limited number of *themes* or *patterns:* i.e., semiotic properties or relations which have emotional significance for a people and which are predicated by that people of many of their activities.[7] Thus, in American culture there are such themes as "success," "efficiency," "progress," and "democracy," not all of which are necessarily consistent with one another.[8]

So pervasive is the role of culture in fixing people's perception and manipulation of natural phenomena that different populations, though occupying the same habitat, may have literally different resources. Indeed, it is only insofar as a habitat has been made valuable by the culturally available beliefs and techniques of a people that it contains any resources at all. As Zimmermann puts it in his functional theory of resources, "Resources *are* not, they *become.*" [9]

In parts of south central Africa, for instance, there are stretches of acid, peaty soils which, when properly drained and treated by wood ash, can produce good crops of millet. The Bemba people, despite perennial hunger, have left these soils unused whereas other peoples, like the Iwa and Inamwanga, have evolved an effective system of exploiting them. So, too, the grassland regions of the American Great Plains, the Argentine pampa, and the Russian steppe literally became a different *ambient*—a different fund of resources—when railroad transportation, as a cultural complex, opened them up to urban markets and led to their conversion from pastoral to farming activities. Likewise, knowledge of genetics, as part of a scientific cultural tradition, can lead to new plant varieties which endow a habitat with altogether different resources. Even political and religious changes may have effects upon the techniques of a population which can reconstitute the resource composition of the habitat.

In the ethnological approach there is an implicit argument which can be stated in the form of a syllogism. First, any resource process, to be adopted, must first be valued (i.e., accorded some worth) by a people in terms of their system of activities.[10] Second, there are some resource complexes which are not valued by a given people in terms of their own system of activities. Therefore, there are some resource complexes which will not be adopted by a given people. In summary form:

Every adoptable set of resource processes will be one which is valued by some population in terms of that population's own system of activities.

There is at least one set of resource processes existing somewhere as a resource complex which is not valued by some population in terms of that population's own system of activities.

Therefore, there is at least one set of resource processes existing somewhere as a resource complex which, for some population, is not an adoptable set of resource processes.

This conclusion yields the set of resource processes which are not adoptable.

The first premise in the argument amounts to a real definition of "adoptable"; as such, it is capable of confirmation or refutation. That it is an empirically true proposition is suggested by the long record of attempts on the part of agricultural extension workers to induce the adoption of improved practices: hybrid corn in Spanish-speaking New Mexico, smaller cattle herds in Kenya, commercial cotton in the Sudan, and manure in much of tropical Africa. The record shows that such attempts have frequently failed or, where they succeeded, were accompanied by skillful reinterpretation of the new practices in terms of a people's own system of activities. Thus, a Lebanese village which had initially resisted the idea of a sanitary, hand pumped water well was eventually persuaded to accept it when the well was identified with the people's religious and family activities. Similarly, in part of French West Africa, farmers were induced to adopt soil conserving contour plowing through an appeal to the people's sense of duty to posterity, that being an important activity in their culture. On the other hand, where a resource process involves beliefs and techniques that are incongruous with a people's system of activities, it will not be adopted by that people, however superior it may be by other criteria.

The minor premise of the argument, that some resource complexes are not valued by some peoples, is amply documented by historical and ethnographic sources. Thus, Arab nomads who conquered North Africa in the seventh century found a resource complex of irrigated commercial agriculture, one which had been operating for centuries under the Roman and Byzantine empires. Instead of adopt-ing it, however, the Arabs supplanted it with their own traditional pastoral complex. In terms of Arab culture, irri-gation was incomprehensible, forest wind breaks were not appreciated, and water lifts in wells were considered objec-tionable.

From the two foregoing premises, we can infer that there are resource complexes existing somewhere which are not adoptable by some other peoples. This conclusion may now be placed alongside the normative proposition, frequently asserted in literature on resource development and con-servation, that *some elements* (practices) of those complexes nevertheless *ought* to be adopted by a given people. The two propositions need not be contradictory. The question arises, however, of determining which resource processes belong together in a resource complex. What criteria does the ethnological approach offer for determining the opti-mum subset of resource processes within the set of adopt-able resource processes?

The answer is to be found in the postulate of *cultural consistency*. A resource process which is consistent, by a people's own modes of reasoning, with important themes or patterns in that people's culture, is more likely to be valued, and hence adopted, than a process which is incon-sistent with those themes. To be sure, there are inconsis-tencies within any culture, indicating that an activity may be valued and adopted by a people even though it is not consistent with any of the themes in their culture. That is, consistency must be regarded as a sufficient though not a necessary condition of the valuation and adoption of a re-source process (or any other activity). As such, it represents an ethnological criterion for specifying an optimum subset of resource processes within the set of adoptable resource processes. In the ethnological approach to resource phenomena, then, the "best" set of resource practices is comprised of those processes which are consistent with the outstanding themes of the whole class of activities comprising a people's culture. A resource complex made up wholly of such processes would be an optimal resource complex.

Such a set of resource processes suggests itself as an appropriate goal for resource planning and policy making. And yet, the existence of inconsistencies and contradictions in all cultures should raise some doubts concerning the wisdom of elevating the criterion of consistency to such primacy. To be sure, if cultural inconsistencies were nothing but anachronisms which invariably faded away with time, governmental policy could well disregard them or even expedite their disappearance. But if, as seems to be the case, there is any kind of gainfulness which such inconsistent resource practices yield to their human agents, we shall have to turn to economic theory for further specifications of an optimum resource complex.

The point of departure for economic theory is the attribute of *scarcity* which attaches to all human activities. This derives from the limited supply in which productive factors, viewed as means to the satisfaction of various wants, are available. Because of scarcity, resource users find themselves confronted with the necessity for choice and, therefore, with the problem of economizing their use of productive factors. To maximize their gainfulness ("want-satisfaction," "utility"), they must combine productive factors in certain proportions rather than others, and they must adopt certain scales of output rather than others. Any resource process which minimizes production costs and maximizes profits will, *ceteris paribus,* be a maximally efficient resource process. Under certain postulated conditions, it will yield a maximum degree of gainfulness to the individual resource users of a population, relative to alternative resource processes.

As a first approximation to economic analysis, then, it is possible to divide a class of adoptable resource processes into two corresponding dichotomies: one, a division into those processes which are privately gainful to individual resource users (in a subjective, psychological sense), and those which are not gainful in this sense; the other, a division into those processes which, given some specified conditions, have at least a formally stated degree of productive efficiency, and those which have less than that degree of productive efficiency.[11] An important argument can then be stated in terms of this simplified schema. First, a gainful set of resource processes is one whose elements (processes) all have not less than a formally stated degree of productive efficiency. Second, there are resource complexes some of whose elements have less than that degree of productive efficiency. Therefore, there are resource complexes which are not gainful. More precisely:

Every gainful set of resource processes will be one each of whose elements (processes) has not less than a formally stated degree of productive efficiency.

There is at least one set of resource processes existing somewhere as a resource complex which contains one or more elements (processes) that, for the members of the population involved, have less than that degree of productive efficiency.

Therefore, there is at least one set of resource processes existing somewhere as a resource complex which, for the members of the population involved, is not a gainful set of resource processes.

This conclusion yields the set of resource processes which are not gainful.

The first premise restricts the use of the term "gainful" to the upper range of a psychological magnitude which, by hypothesis, corresponds to those degrees of productive efficiency which have not less than some formally stated value. That the definition represents a true proposition is suggested by entrepreneurial behavior in various fields of resource exploitation. Farm management research, for instance, has shown that, with prices given, some commercial farmers do combine productive factors in proportions that will minimize their costs. As a result, the resource practices of those farmers are maximally efficient and are therefore gainful to them. Commercial fishermen, too, show a high order of inventive ingenuity in adapting their fishing gear, their vessels, and their range of operations to varying market conditions and varying supplies of fish. By virtue of this versatility, their resource practices tend to be maximally efficient and therefore gainful to them.

In regard to the minor premise of the argument, there are any number of resource complexes, some of whose elements (processes) have less than a formally stated degree of productive efficiency. Feudal agriculture, for instance, typically binds productive factors to fixed proportions. It thus commits its human agents to some practices which may not be as efficient as alternative processes involving a different proportioning of productive factors. Among the Rowanduz Kurds, for instance, there has been a recent trend toward the cultivation of tobacco as a cash crop. This trend points toward a more efficient combination of productive factors, so far as profit making is concerned. Yet tobacco cultivation requires an arrangement of land holdings which is out of keeping with the scattered, fragmented character of traditional Kurdish land division. A lag has thus been introduced into the process of conversion from subsistence agriculture to cash crop agriculture. Anachronistic elements of a feudal resource complex persist even though they are not as efficient as those involved in commercial tobacco farming. So, too, in Cyprus, until 1946, different productive factors—buildings, trees, fields, water rights, etc.—could be legally inherited by different individuals even though these units all occupied the same parcel of land. The resulting maze of legal rights to these resources impaired their free substitution for one another in response to opportunities for profit. Again, the effect was an inhibition of more efficient resource processes by less efficient ones.

From these two premises the conclusion follows that there are resource complexes which are not privately gainful to individuals in the social orders concerned. It is this fact, along with certain discrepancies between private and collective gainfulness, which provides the animus to much of contemporary resource planning and policy making. In many countries, the avowed objective of government is to encourage the adoption of gainful resource practices. Given this normative commitment, the question now arises: is there an economically optimum subset of resource processes within the set of gainful resource processes? Is there, in other words, a class of *most* gainful resource processes? Such an optimum, if definable, might supposedly serve as a rationale for the planned development and conservation of natural resources.

One optimum to which economic theory points is that of the rational allocation of resources in a free, competitive market economy. In this conceptual model, productive factors are assumed to be freely substitutable for one another, in the sense that it is always possible to replace one input by another (e.g., land by labor) in achieving a desired level of output. Given this fundamental assumption, with a number of formally stated conditions, it can be shown that there is always one allocation of productive factors which will minimize cost and maximize profit. At this point, the gainfulness of resource users (viewed now as a continuous variable rather than as a dichotomy) is maximized.

Two of the necessary (though not sufficient) conditions underlying this model are as follows: (a) For any level of output there will be some point at which total cost is minimized; such a least cost condition exists when productive factors have been so combined that the ratios of their respective prices are equal to the ratios of their "marginal products" (the change in total product resulting from a unit increment of that factor); (b) There will be one determinate level of output at which total profits are maximized or losses minimized; such an output exists when "marginal revenue" (the change in total revenue resulting from a unit increase in output sold) is equal to "marginal cost" (the change in total cost resulting from that unit increase in output). A resource complex whose component processes answer this description will be an optimum one by the criterion of efficiency. Under any other subset of processes, it will always be possible to enhance the economic value of a population's total output of goods, and therewith the gainfulness of those goods to individuals, by recombining productive factors or by changing the level of output.[12]

Economic theory thus defines a subset of optimum resource processes within the more inclusive set of gainful resource processes. A resource complex made up wholly of such processes would seem to be an appropriate goal for resource planning and policy making. If, in addition, such a goal were to coincide with the goals implied in the ecological and the ethnological approaches, it would offer an even surer criterion for resource development and conservation. There would then be no difficulty whatever in rationalizing governmental efforts at promoting particular resource processes and discouraging others, so long as the outcome were a set of practices lying within the three coinciding optima—those of ecology, ethnology and economics. Yet the assumption of the present study has been that there are structural features to people's use of resources which limit the scope of voluntary action on the part of government and resource users alike. Is such an assumption consistent with the view that resource planning and policy making can and should be aimed at simultaneously realizing three different kinds of optima?

An answer to this question cannot be given until we have first established a question of fact: is it true that in every social order a coincidence exists in the three subsets of optimum resource processes such that these subsets share identical elements (resource processes)? Is it true, in other words, that in every social order the ecological, ethnological, and economic optima are equivalent? This, of course, is an empirical question which can only be settled by an appeal to cases. It is a matter which is going to occupy us in the chapter which follows.

Thus far in our study, though, we have established three important propositions. We have established the fact that for any given people and any given habitat: (1) there are certain resource complexes which are not *possible;* (2) there are other resource complexes which are not *adoptable;* (3) there are other resource complexes which are not *gainful.* These are the conclusions to which our three syllogisms—the ecological, the ethnological and the economic—have led us. Their truth has been further confirmed by empirical considerations. We may regard the three propositions, then, as established facts. Corresponding to them we may define three sets of resource processes, each with its logical complement, viz., those which are:

Possible,	Not possible
Adoptable,	Not adoptable
Gainful,	Not gainful

Together these sets comprise a universe of resource processes within which any resource complex can be located.

NOTES

* Aristotle, *Ethica nicomachea,* ed. and trans. W. D. Ross (Oxford: the Clarendon Press, 1925), Bk. I, chap. viii.

1. Indeed, not all ecologists would subscribe to the approach here designated as ecological, nor would all ethnologists or economists subscribe to the approaches here designated as ethnological and economic, respectively.

2. That is, "possible in the long run."

3. Carl O. Sauer, "The Agency of Man on the Earth," in William L. Thomas, Jr. (ed.), *Man's Role in Changing the Face of the Earth* (Chicago: University of Chicago Press, 1956), p. 49.

4. A. G. Tansley, *The British Islands and their Vegetation* (Cambridge: Cambridge University Press, 1939), pp. 224-25. Cf. the equivalent concept "disclimax" which is employed by some ecologists, e.g., Eugene P. Odum, *Fundamentals of Ecology* (Philadelphia: W. B. Saunders Co., 1953), p. 199.

5. Raymond Furon, *L'érosion du sol* (Paris: Payot, 1947), p. 210. My translation.

6. Reprinted from "Cultural Differences in the Interpretation of Natural Resources," by Alexander Spoehr, in William L. Thomas, Jr. (ed), *Man's Role in Changing the Face of the Earth,* by permission of The University of Chicago Press. Copyright 1956 by The University of Chicago.

7. Albert K. Cohen, "On the Place of 'Themes' and Kindred Concepts in Social Theory," *American Anthropologist,* L (1948), 436-43; Morris Edward Opler, "Themes as Dynamic Forces in Culture," *American Journal of Sociology,* LI (1945), 198-206; Ruth Benedict, *Patterns of Culture* (Boston: Houghton Mifflin Co., 1934).

8. Robin M. Williams, Jr., *American Society* (New York: Alfred A. Knopf, Inc., 1951), chap. xi.

9. Erich W. Zimmermann, *World Resources and Industries* (rev. ed.; New York: Harper and Bros., 1951), p. 15.

10. "A value is a conception, explicit or implicit, distinctive of an individual or characteristic of a group, of the desirable which influences the selection from available modes, means, and ends of action." Clyde Kluckhohn and others, "Values and Value-Orientations in the Theory of Action," in Talcott Parsons and Edward A. Shils, *Toward a General Theory of Action* (Cambridge, Mass.: Harvard University Press, 1951), p. 395.

11. Regarding the correspondence which we have here defined between *subjective* gainfulness and *objective* efficiency, we must emphasize that the psychological content of "gainful" and "nongainful" has been deliberately left unspecified. We are only asserting that there are two empirically nonempty sets of subjective phenomena, having their locus in the minds of individual resource users, one of them corresponding to productively efficient resource processes, the other of them corresponding to productively inefficient resource processes, and we are designating these two sets, respectively, as "gainful" and "nongainful" resource processes.

12. See, for instance: Kenneth E. Boulding, *Economic Analysis* (New York: Harper and Bros., 1941), chaps. xx-xxiii; Paul A. Samuelson, *Economics* (New York: McGraw-Hill Book Co., 1948), chaps. xxi-xxii.

CHAPTER III

DIFFERENCES
AMONG RESOURCE OPTIMA

Die 'Harmonie', die so vielfach in
der Landschaft gesucht und ge-
funden wird, ist weniger häufig als
man glauben möchte. Mensch und
Natur stehen in einem dialekt-
ischen Verhältnis, das sich nur in
besonderen Situationen 'harmo-
nisch' ausgleicht.

MARTIN SCHWIND [1]

I F RESOURCE PLANS and policies are to be anything more
than opportunistic ventures, if they are to cohere with
other objectives of government, they must have some theoretical rationale. They must, in other words, appear as
instances of propositions which together form a logically
closed system of thought that embraces the whole range of
governmental activity. Suppose it were to be shown, now,
that any resource program which aimed at equating marginal costs and marginal revenues would perforce be

compatible with both anthropogenic climax and cultural consistency. Such coherence with three distinct criteria of optimum resource processes—ecological, ethnological, and economic—would make the program a presumptively rational course for governmental action.

If, however, a social order were to exist in which the pursuit of one of these optima excluded realizing one or both of the other optima, the reflective policy maker will be in a quandary. To rationalize any resource program, he will then have to make an arbitrary choice as between ecological, ethnological, and economic criteria, or else he will have to strike some sort of balance among them. Failing either of these alternatives, he will have to disavow a rational justification of his program and fall back upon *ad hoc* justifications (which, of course, might be quite sufficient for political purposes). On the supposition, however, that existential pressures may constrain a planner or policy maker to seek some logically grounded rationale for his program, let us face up to our problem. Let us see if we can find a social order in which the three optimum subsets of resource processes, as described in the preceding chapter, do *not* coincide.

In terms of method, our problem is one of finding a case which falsifies the universally quantified statement that:

| The set of ecologically optimal resource processes | coincides with | The set of ethnologically optimal resource processes | coincides with | The set of economically optimal resource processes |

Any such method, which rests on the single case rather than on a frequency distribution of cases, will allow only a negative sort of proof. It will allow only the refutation, not the confirmation, of a universally quantified proposition. The conclusion which it yields, however, is a compelling one, and for our present purposes, it is all we shall need.

Prudence, of course, will dictate the choice of some case which is not obviously "loaded" with respect to the issue at hand, and about which sufficient information—ecological, ethnological and economic—is available. On both counts the Tiv people of Benue province, Nigeria, afford an appropriate case. The Tiv are subsistence farmers whose resource complex involves hoe cultivation and bush fallow. These practices are well suited to tropical soil conditions; in principle, if not in practice, they would admit of a stable equilibrium *vis-à-vis* the organic and physical environment of east-central Nigeria. Moreover, the Tiv culture, while complicated in certain respects, does not have the rigid structure which characterizes some cultures. Rather, it consists of a limited number of themes which are associated with, but not implicated by, one another, thus presenting fewer resistances to the valuing and adoption of certain kinds of new resource processes than might be the case. Finally, the Tiv have shown a fair degree of resilience in adapting their resource practices to various exigencies. This versatility in substituting units of certain productive factors for units of others has allowed them the possibility of increasing the efficiency by which to overcome the attribute of scarcity attaching to their cultural activities.

The Tiv case, in other words, does not rashly prejudge the problem with which we are presently concerned. Moreover, it is a case about which pertinent and reliable information is available. The description and analysis which the

Bohannans have made of Tiv culture yields precisely the kind of data which are called for by our present problem—that of determining how the three optimal subsets of resource processes are related to each other. In the discussion which follows we shall draw our empirical materials very largely from the ethnographic studies of the Bohannans.[2]

Tiv resource practices are based on a type of bush fallow which is employed over much of Nigeria. In this system, the fields are rotated rather than the crops, with the result that only a limited proportion of land can be cultivated at any one time, the remainder being fallow until its fertility is restored. The Tiv have built into their system of bush fallow two distinct sets of practices: (1) that of southern Nigeria, which is based on the planting of yams, cassava, and other root crops, and (2) that of northern Nigeria, which is based on the growing of guinea corn, millet, and other cereals.[3] These two sets of practices appear as phases in a more or less typical cropping cycle: newly cleared land is first planted in yams; second-year fields are planted in millet and guinea corn; third-year fields, supposedly fallow, are often planted in beniseed, cassava, and other side crops.[4]

The first of these phases begins in August with the communal pulling of the grass which has grown wild during the fallow period. As this operation gets under way, the farms of the various members of a compound (a group of huts) are laid out. The male residents of the compound then hoe rows of earthen heaps or mounds, working up the topsoil. In February, seed yams are planted in these mounds, both men and women co-operating in the work. Various extra crops—cassava, beans, peanuts, etc.—are also planted in the yam fields. In December and January, the yams are harvested by women. Weeding and cultivating is done entirely by women. By spring, the old mounds are levelled by the men. Then, with the onset of heavy spring rains, the men sow millet seed and work the soil slightly. Various other crops are interplanted with millet—cassava, beniseed, and especially guinea corn, the latter being planted somewhat later than the others. Millet and guinea corn are harvested in June and December, respectively, after which the field is considered fallow. Many Tiv then plant beniseed, cassava, and other side crops on their "fallow" fields, first burning the grass and mixing the ashes with the soil. Land will remain in fallow for varying numbers of years, depending on the soil type. Ideally, the land is not cleared again until certain kinds of grasses have appeared which indicate to Tiv that an adequate restoration of soil fertility has occurred. Actually, however, population densities have become so great that, particularly among the southern Tiv, land is in almost continuous cultivation.[5]

It is this circumstance which gives rise to questions of policy. In the Tiv view, *nya kuma ga:* "the land is not sufficient." [6] The government, Tiv believe, has denied them access to land which is legitimately theirs by restricting their growing population to a fixed territory marked by boundaries. In the government view, on the other hand, the Tiv appear reluctant to migrate to areas where land could be had in abundance; likewise, they seem unwilling to adopt green manuring and other soil building processes. Both views—that of the Tiv and that of the government—are, in a sense, correct. Both, however, rest on different assumptions as to desirable resource policy.

Let us turn now to the theories which have been outlined

in the last chapter—the ecological, the ethnological and the economic—and look at Tiv resource practices from these three points of view. Let us further consider what would be the optimum resource processes for Tiv people given the criteria formulated in these three approaches. After this, we shall turn to the main problem of our chapter and determine whether or not the ecological, ethnological, and economic optima are indeed identical.

In terms of ecological criteria, Tiv resource practices are not in equilibrium with the organic and physical environment. They are therefore not permanent. The part of Nigeria which is now occupied by the Tiv is characterized by a light, sandy soil, somewhat acid in character. Prior to Tiv occupation it was probably covered with savanna forest and, in some places, with a denser forest growth. Today, practically none of this early forest growth is left. Overcultivation has placed such heavy demands on the land that secondary growth of woody vegetation is impossible. The fallow period in Tiv territory is sometimes as short as two years, and is quite inadequate for the maintenance of soil structure and fertility. Insufficient organic matter is being returned to the soil, the soil texture is being impaired, and gully erosion has appeared. Land in fallow is quickly preempted by grasses which grow from rhizomes.[7] A particularly hardy spear grass has succeeded the more soil building grasses and, along with a low bush growth, dominates the Tiv landscape. Not only does this spear grass fail to rehabilitate the land during its brief fallow period but it persists into the next cultivation period as a weed which impairs crop yields.[8]

Attaining anthropogenic climax would clearly require,

first and foremost, a lengthening of the fallow period. Of this fact the Tiv are, in their own terms, fully aware.[9] Indeed, bush fallow agriculture, properly managed, could be a system well suited to the conservation of tropical soils. Tiny patches of cultivated land on which various crops have been interplanted, all maturing at different times so as to afford continuous plant cover for the soil, and surrounded by a wall of bush through which topsoil cannot wash away, are well contrived to preserve the capability of tropical land.[10] Anthropogenic climax would require only the establishing of a regenerative bush fallow. Such a fallow would represent, for this land, an ecologically optimum subset within the set of possible resource processes. Such is the policy goal to which ecological theory would point.

The ethnological optimum is a rather different one. In Tiv culture, as analyzed by Bohannan, two themes are particularly important to the people's resource practices. One is the ascription to every kinsman of a right to a fair share of land. The other is the assessment of personal relationships in terms of genealogical nearness or distance. These are semiotic relations which Tiv predicate of the activities that comprise their resource complex. Both figure in a characteristically Tiv man-land relationship in which the farms of any one individual or group shift from one cropping cycle to the next, maintaining, however, certain stable spatial arrangements.

To begin with, Tiv do not recognize any rights to particular sites. They only recognize rights to positions, to particular arrangements of people over space. Under this system, every woman has an acknowledged right to enough land to provide for herself and her children, and every man has an acknowledged right to enough land on which to prepare farms for his wives (Tiv are polygynous). A woman derives her land rights from marriage; a husband derives his by filiation from his "minimal segment," i.e., from the smallest segment of his father's lineage to which a discrete territorial block of land can be associated. Specifically a man has a right to *some* group of farms that will be located on whatever land his full brothers (those having the same mother) are currently cultivating. The size of his farms will vary with his needs, or rather with those of his wives and children. A wife who has many children will receive a larger farm than a wife who has few children. A man's current "allotment" will thus depend on the size of his family; it will vary from one cropping cycle to the next as his own and his brothers' families grow or decline in size.

Under such a system, farms can have no fixed boundaries. Over a period of years, the lands which are cultivated by any one man and his wives will shift, so that few individuals are able to remember precisely where they may have farmed ten years before. In the absence of any central authority—power is remarkably decentralized among the Tiv—disputes are bound to arise as to who will occupy what sites. And, in fact, land disputes are a ubiquitous feature of the Tiv economy. As a man's farms expand to meet the needs of his growing family, or as his brothers' farms press upon his, he will be driven to clear fields in fallow land that is claimed by someone else. To meet this exigency, the Tiv have evolved a standard formula: a man (or group of kinsmen) will always expand his fields into the fallow of whatever neighbor is most distant of kin.

This, in fact, is a moral injunction. It is bound up with

the other theme of Tiv culture to which reference has been made, viz., the assessment of personal relationships in terms of genealogical nearness or distance. The nearer that any two Tiv are to one another genealogically, the more solidary their relationships with each other are supposed to be. It is mandatory that one be, or at least appear to be, solidary with one's full brothers. Half brothers are one step removed, genealogically; yet in issues concerning remoter kinsmen, they are expected to be solidary. Cousins (sons of one's father's brother) are still further removed; but in issues concerning still remoter kinsmen, they, too, are expected to be solidary. Social interaction and group formation become more intense with genealogical nearness; [11] thus, work groups, such as men hoeing their fields, will most often be composed of brothers, particularly of full brothers.

When a man wishes to expand his farms, then, he will clear fallow nearest whichever of his neighbors is most distantly related to him genealogically. His point of view, Bohannan observes, is expressed in these words: "Would you cause hunger in the compound of your mother's son (*wanggo,* a close relative) if you can get land from your father's son (*wanter,* a more distant relative?)" [12] In a similar fashion, every lineage group will expand its aggregate of farms against those of whatever neighboring lineage group is most distantly related to it genealogically. The net result is a topological arrangement of farms which "migrate" over space, somewhat like the patches on a rubber sheet that one might stretch in some direction, with all the parts maintaining the same relative position to one another. Different lineage segments preserve, as it were, a topologically invariant relationship with one another over space, though their respective holdings are forever changing hands.

In actual fact, these two themes of Tiv culture are not fully realized. Population densities among the southern Tiv are so great that individuals cannot make as large farms as they need; there is not enough land to go around. The process of expansion which Tiv consider to be normal has thus been arrested. Yet the themes persist.[13] So long as they do, the ethnological criterion of a resource optimum is unmistakable: continued (or resumed) expansion of the fields of individuals and lineage groups into the fallow lands of genealogically most distant kinsmen. This is the "solution" which Tiv themselves see. It is clearly consistent with two of their basic cultural themes: the ascription, to every kinsman, of a right to a fair share of land, and the assessment of personal relationships in terms of genealogical nearness or distance. As such, it represents the ethnologically optimum subset within the set of adoptable resource processes.

Consider now the economic optimum. As already indicated, the Tiv have shown a certain degree of flexibility in adapting their resource practices to changing circumstances. Improved transportation has brought the Tiv more and more into a market economy; this in its turn has led to changes in the people's cropping practices. Moreover, Tiv men are given to a great deal of travelling, trading, and working for wages, over much of West Africa. Finally, population pressure among the southern Tiv has led to shorter fallow, smaller fields, a greater proportion of land in actual cultivation, and changed proportions among the various crops.[14] In these respects there is a very evident substitutability of productive factors (land and labor) as between different enterprises. The Tiv, by shifting factors from one enterprise to another, have managed to increase the efficiency by which they realize their subsistence needs.

The adoption of cash crops further illustrates the Tiv propensity to economize their use of productive factors. Over a period of some thirty years, the Tiv have been growing beniseed for European trading companies. In the last ten years, they have added soybeans and rice to their repertoire of cash crops.[15] There is also a nearby cash market for cassava.[16] This partial involvement in a market economy has greatly increased the demand for land and, at the same time, has reduced the output of staple crops like millet and guinea corn.[17] It has, as a result, aggravated the ecological imbalance which characterizes the Tiv habitat.

Despite the resilience of Tiv resource practices, there are some limits to the proportions with which productive factors can be combined. Tiv are reluctant, for instance, to move as isolated family groups into remote areas of greater land abundance. The direction and distance of Tiv migration is dictated by kinship organization rather than by economic opportunity. Moreover, the Tiv are unwilling to adopt leguminous green manures in their cropping cycle, and they are equally resistant to compost heaps. Rights to land are nonexchangeable and unalienable, and they are independent of a man's relative competence and diligence. Such fixities in factor combinations set an upper limit to the degree of efficiency which the Tiv may attain in their resource practices.

The attainment of an economically optimum set of resource processes would, of course, require the dissolution of all culturally imposed limits to the free substitution of productive factors for one another. It would involve a full fledged market economy, in which the participants, ever responsive to varying exchange opportunities, could freely shift units of various factors of production from one enterprise to another. With continuous substitution between factors, it would then be possible to realize those factor combinations which equated marginal costs and marginal revenues. At this point, a *most* gainful set of resource processes would exist. Such a subset, within the more inclusive set of gainful resource processes, would represent an economic optimum. This is the policy goal to which economic theory points.

Three resource optima have now been specified for the Tiv people and their habitat. These optima have been formulated in terms of three distinct theories concerning natural resources: the ecological, the ethnological, and the economic. By way of summary identification, the three optima may be represented as follows:

The ecological optimum: a regenerative bush fallow.
The ethnological optimum: expansion of fields along kinship lines.
The economic optimum: a free market economy.

If we reflect, now, on our general problem, we may again ask ourselves: do these three optimum sets of resource processes have identical elements? Could there be, for the Tiv, a conjoint attainment of regenerative bush fallow, expansion of fields along kinship lines, and a free market economy? Would these be compatible policy goals for the planned development and conservation of Tiv resources?

It will be sufficient to consider the question with respect to two issues: land allocation and population movement. These are fundamental to so many other issues in the Tiv situation that conclusions concerning them will have general application. What, then, would a regenerative bush fallow entail with regard to land allocation?—with regard to population movement? Are these consequences the same as those which would be entailed by expansion of fields along kinship lines?—by a free market economy? The following table will summarize the pertinent information:

	With regard to *Land Allocation*	*With regard to* *Population Movement*
Regenerative bush fallow would entail:	A smaller proportion of land in crops at any one time (larger proportion in fallow), and a smaller proportion of cash crops relative to staple crops (owing to the intensified demand for land which cash crops create).	"Leap-frog" migration by discrete individuals and family groups to less densely populated areas of Tiv territory (involving topological rearrangement of groups).
Expansion of fields along kinship lines would entail:	Little or no change in present proportions between crop land and fallow land and between cash crops and staple crops (owing to pressure of population on available land among southern Tiv).	"Encroachment" migration by lineage groups onto fallow lands of most distant kin (involving maintenance of present topological arrangement of groups).
Free market economy would entail:	A larger proportion of land in crops at any one time and a larger proportion of cash crops relative to staple crops (the short-time horizon of Tiv culture precludes "investment conservation" in which marginal costs and marginal revenues might be equated as between the present and a remoter future).	"Leap-frog" migration by discrete individuals and family groups to less densely populated areas of Tiv territory (thus dissolving present fixities in land-labor factor combinations).

Divergence between the three optima is evident from this table. Apparently, for the Tiv, at least, the three optimum sets of resource processes do not have identical elements. Any attempt to achieve, say, anthropogenic climax (by establishing a regenerative bush fallow) would violate the conditions of cultural consistency (which calls for expansion of fields along kinship lines) and of equated marginal costs and marginal revenues (which calls for a free market economy). Likewise, any attempt to achieve either of the other two optima would violate the conditions of the remaining two optima. Only on one issue, that of population movement, do two of the optima coincide, viz., the ecological and the economic. These optima diverge, however, in respect to the other issue, that of land allocation.

As a universal proposition, then, the assertion that:

The set of ecologically optimal resource processes	*coincides with*	The set of ethnologically optimal resource processes	*coincides with*	The set of economically optimal resource processes

cannot be sustained. This negative finding is a most important one. It obviously complicates the task of finding a generalized rationale for any kind of resource planning and policy making. Governmental intervention in the use of natural resources is hardly to be justified on the grounds of a supposed identity in ecological, ethnological, and economic criteria of optimum resource use.

Several alternatives still remain open to the resource planner. He can choose one particular criterion of resource optima, disregarding the other two, and then base his entire rationale upon that criterion alone. Such an arbitrary choice, however, would require its own rationale. Alternatively, the resource planner can forego a rational justification of his endeavors and simply draw on *ad hoc* principles to account for his activities. Finally, he can retain all three criteria of resource optima and look for some method of balancing them off against each other. The first two alternatives would presumably vitiate the whole point of the present study by renouncing any possibility of a generalized theoretical rationale for resource planning and policy making. Only the third of them, then, would seem to call for any further consideration. Let us turn to it, therefore, and ask ourselves the same question with which we closed the previous chapter: what relationship do the optimum subsets of resource processes have to one another? If they are not coincident with one another are they perhaps *extrema* "magnitudes" of the three properties of possibility, adoptability, and gainfulness? In this event the question would become one of locating a resource complex with reference to the three sets: the possible, the adoptable, and the gainful, of which the three optima are *extrema* subsets.

NOTES

1. Martin Schwind, "Sinn und Ausdruck der Landschaft," *Studium Generale*, III (1950), 198.
2. Paul Bohannan, *Tiv Farm and Settlement* (London: Her Majesty's Stationery Office, 1954); Laura and Paul Bohannan, *The Tiv of Central Nigeria* ("Ethnographic Survey of Africa, Western Africa" [(London: International African Institute, 1953]), Part VIII; Paul Bohannan, "The Migration and Expansion of the Tiv," *Africa*, XXIV (1954), 2-16; Paul Bohannan, "Some Principles of Exchange and Investment among the Tiv," *American Anthropologist*, LVII (1955), 60-70.

3. Bohannan, *The Tiv* . . . , p. 52; see also: K. M. Buchanan and J. C. Pugh, *Land and People in Nigeria* (London: University of London Press, 1955), pp. 105-7.

4. See the schematic analysis of these phases in Bohannan, *Tiv Farm* . . . , p. 22.

5. Bohannan, *Tiv Farm* . . . , pp. 15-21; see also: G. W. G. Briggs, "Soil Deterioration in the Southern Districts of Tiv Division, Benue Province," *Farm and Forest,* II (1941), 9-10.

6. Bohannan, *Tiv Farm* . . . , p. 10. By permission of the Controller of Her Britannic Majesty's Stationery Office.

7. Pierre Gourou, *The Tropical World* (New York: Longmans, Green and Co. Ltd., 1953), p. 41.

8. On the generality of this problem over much of the African continent, see *ibid.*

9. Bohannan, *Tiv Farm* . . . , p. 47.

10. L. Dudley Stamp, "Land Utilization and Soil Erosion in Nigeria," *Geographical Review,* XXVIII (1938).

11. Bohannan, *The Tiv* . . . , p. 20.

12. Bohannan, *Tiv Farm* . . . , p. 32. By permission of the Controller of Her Britannic Majesty's Stationery Office.

13. *Ibid.,* pp. 58-59; Bohannan, "The Migration and Expansion . . . ," pp. 4-5.

14. Bohannan, *Tiv Farm* . . . , pp. 47-49 .

15. Bohannan, *The Tiv* . . . , pp. 14, 53.

16. Bohannan, *Tiv Farm* . . . , p. 30.

17. *Ibid.,* pp. 15, 48, 58; Bohannan, *The Tiv* . . . , p. 57.

CHAPTER IV

THE RANGE AND LIMITS
OF A RESOURCE COMPLEX

> It is a characteristic of the culture
> pattern once launched to demand
> its own expression at any cost what-
> ever to the environment.
>   PAUL B. SEARS[1]

JUSTIFICATIONS for one or another resource policy are commonly stated with little regard for their logical derivation. Indeed, they are almost never derived from other propositions by formal rules of reasoning. Practical politics impose no such requirement upon spokesmen for resource policies. As a result, propositions are frequently asserted which, in a logical analysis, would commit their speakers to assumptions concerning the social order that are patently false.

When serious proposals are advanced, then, to change or to maintain particular resource practices, it should not be out of place to look into their axiomatic grounds. What assumptions concerning the nature of resource processes and the social order underlie them? What assumptions, for instance, are tacitly made by the ecologist who suggests that natives in South Africa be bound to the land while a small landlord elite impose better resource practices upon them, all for the sake of conserving the soil? [2] Conversely, what is assumed by the economist who views with equanimity the mining of topsoil and its conversion to desert, noting that in a commercial economy ". . . we can afford to do this"? [3] Would either of these sets of implicit assumptions square with the actual character of a resource complex?

In point of fact, these two normative propositions are candid versions of two sharply contrasting theories of resource processes and the social order, both of which are widely current in the literature on natural resources. One is the somewhat utopian notion that a resource complex can be freely fashioned to answer the purposes of an ideal, such as conservation of the soil. The other is the more pragmatic notion that a resource complex need only be gainful to be viable.

The point can be stated more precisely: There are certain resource policy proposals which, if traced back logically to their premises, rest on the assumption that, in any social order, the elements of a resource complex can lie wholly *outside* the set of gainful resource processes. It is enough that they be possible or, perhaps, that they be adoptable; beyond this, resource practices are subject to no dictates from the social order. On the other hand, there are other resource policy proposals which, if traced back to their logical origins, presuppose that, in any social order, the elements of a resource complex must lie wholly *inside* the set of gainful resource processes. It is not enough that they be physically possible and culturally adoptable; they must be economically gainful as well. Each of these two conceptions of resource practices may be taken as a universally quantified proposition, in the sense that each is held to be descriptive of any resource complex as it is or could be.

At this point, our problem becomes an empirical one. Can we find a social order in which *neither* of the two foregoing hypotheses is true? Can we find a social order, that is, in which the elements of a resource complex lie both in the set of gainful resource processes and in the set of nongainful resource processes? Even more, is this set of resource practices a viable one? What are the limits of its viability? As in our preceding chapter, we must select a reasonable case in which the possible truth of one or the other of the hypotheses is not excluded *ex ante*. Furthermore, whatever case we select must allow an unequivocal assignment of resource practices to one or the other of the complementary sets: gainful processes and nongainful processes. In the absence of quantitative economic data bearing on the efficiency of resource processes for any but a few Western lands, there is no possibility of finding a social order in which a precise cutting point between the gainful and the nongainful can be defined. The difficulty of finding a reasonable case would seem to be insurmountable.

We have chosen a particular way out of this impasse. We have selected a case in which the forces of social change are prominently exhibited. By examining trends over time and noting such phenomena as "innovations," "adaptations," and "experiments," we should be able to identify those resource practices, if any, which unmistakably lie within the set of gainful processes—those which are sufficiently high on a scale of efficiency as to be clearly gainful. Likewise, by examining trends over time, and noting such phenomena as "survivals," "anomalies," and "contradictions," we should be able to discern fairly well those resource practices, if any, which unmistakably lie within the set of nongainful processes—those which are sufficiently low on a scale of efficiency to be clearly nongainful.

The case we have chosen is from the northeastern plateau area of Northern Rhodesia. In this area, population movements over the past, and industrialization at the present, have subjected the resource practices of several peoples to continuous change. Older practices are juxtaposed with new ones in a way that should afford a clear answer to the question of whether the elements of a resource complex always lie within the gainful set or within the nongainful set, or whether, contrary to the two foregoing hypotheses, they may lie within both sets simultaneously. The plateau of Northern Rhodesia has been surveyed by ecologists, ethnologists, and agricultural economists, with the result that a wealth of dependable information is at hand relative to our problem. In particular, the ecological reports of Trapnell and Clothier, and the ethnographic studies of Richards, Whiteley, Allan, and Peters provide the kind of data which is necessary for judging the universal truth of the hypotheses presently at issue.[4]

Existing resource complexes in northeastern Rhodesia are variants of one basic complex, the *citemene* system. This same complex is known variously as the *ladang* in Java, *caingin* in the Philippines, *ray* in Vietnam, *milpa* in

Mexico, and *conuco* in Venezuela. Its essential feature is the clearing of a patch of land in the forest, followed by burning of the branches and vegetation. An ash fertilized bed results which is then planted to a crop. After one or several croppings, the land reverts to forest and a new clearing is made, and village sites follow the route of successive clearings thus made in the forest.[5]

This complex of shifting agriculture has proven to be peculiarly suited to tropical soil conditions and to peoples whose culture affords only the simplest of tools. *Citemene* agriculture, for instance, permits use of the poor sandy soils which prevail over most of northeastern Rhodesia, a land whose agricultural possibilities have been further limited by an extremely seasonal distribution of rainfall.[6] The *citemene* complex involves only an axe and a hoe. Its labor requirements are low and its crop yields are dependable.[7] Its demands upon the land, to be sure, are heavy. In order to get enough ash for a fertile seed bed, the *citemene* complex requires the clearing of an area many times larger than that which is to be cropped. Enormous tracts of woodland are thus necessary for the support of a comparatively small population. After a brief period of cultivation, the land has then to rest for some thirty years or more if there is to be adequate regeneration of trees. Unfortunately, the pressure of population upon the land has become so great in the Rhodesias that actual regeneration is considerably less than this.[8] An ecological succession through scrub forest, bush, and eventually grassland has resulted, with an obvious reduction in the land's long run carrying capacity. The process of burning, too, is destructive of nitrogen and organic matter, though it does have the beneficial effect of adding phosphate and potash to the soil as well as of correcting the land's excessive acidity.[9]

Let us consider now in some detail the *citemene* complex as it operates among the Bemba, who are today the largest single tribe in northeastern Rhodesia. In our account, we shall employ the present tense to describe Bemba *citemene* practices, our intent being to portray the complex in its original and essential form. Later in the chapter, we shall see that some of these practices have been modified by the contemporary industrial transformation of Central Africa.

At the beginning of the tree cutting season, the men of a Bemba village will decide just which strips of woodland they are going to clear for their respective millet gardens. Each such clearing, once made, will belong to the man who clears it, and the crops he grows on it will be his and his family's.[10] Religious rites which are centered at the house of the village headman inaugurate the tree cutting operation. These ceremonies invoke the help of ancestral spirits and articulate a system of political authority which is distinctive to the Bemba tribe.[11] Tree cutting itself is a highly valued activity, associated in the people's minds with skill and manliness.[12] The Bemba consider their technique of tree cutting, which involves pollarding the trees rather than cutting them close to the ground, to be superior to that of neighboring peoples.[13] The practical object of the tree cutting is to provide each man with a maximum amount of brushwood and branches with which to fertilize his garden. This material is stacked in the center of one's clearing and is burned in late October or early November, yielding a more or less circular ash-fertilized bed in which finger millet is sown following the first rains.[14] Other crops, par-

ticularly gourds, kaffir corn, and cassava are usually interplanted with the millet.[15] Cultivation of the crop is unnecessary, and by May, it is ready to be reaped.[16] Prayer,
with offerings of food and cloth to the ancestral spirits, ac-
companies the harvest. In the following year, new clearings
are made in the woodland and the process is repeated. Over
a period of four or five years, the clearings have to be made
further and further away from the village. When most of
the accessible woodland has been depleted, the village is
relocated, and the sequence begins all over again at the new
site.

As successively new clearings are made in the woodland,
the old ones are planted to secondary crops, in sequences
that will vary somewhat from village to village. Generally,
during the second year the old millet gardens are planted
to groundnuts; in the third year they are sown again to
finger millet; in the fourth year the land is dug up into
mounds and is planted to beans; and by the fifth or sixth
year the land has become so thoroughly exhausted that it is
allowed to revert to bush.[17] Mounds, too, are employed for
the cultivation of legumes, cassava, sweet potatoes, and
kaffir corn. These are made not only in the old millet gardens out in the bush but also in the immediate village
environs. The preparation of mounds always involves la-
borious hoeing, which the Bemba people dislike; yet without them, there could be none of the supplementary crops
which are so necessary to the Bemba diet.[18]

Variations on the *citemene* complex consist principally
of the arrangement of garden beds within the cleared woodland and of the particular succession of crops that are
planted after the first year. Among the Lala, a tribe living

to the south of the Bemba, usually several small millet gardens are planted within each cleared area, rather than a single garden as among the Bemba. Also, after a single year's use the Lala gardens are generally abandoned rather than being planted to subsequent crops.[19] This variant of the *citemene* complex is even more extravagant in its demands upon the forest than the Bemba system. To save labor in carrying branches and brushwood, the Lala prefer to stack this material in several small piles rather than, as do the Bemba, in a single larger pile. This practice gives rise to their numerous small millet gardens within a single clearing, each of which will unavoidably have some waste border around its circumference on which nothing can grow. The aggregate of this waste border is far greater than in the Bemba system, with the result that the Lala destroy much more woodland for each acre of cultivated land than do the Bemba.[20] Moreover, the difficulty of tending innumerable small patches of land accounts for the Lala's tendency to abandon a site after one year's cultivation rather than to plant it to other crops as do the Bemba.[21] Overpopulation has further aggravated the situation. Forest regrowth can barely get under way before the immature trees must be cut down to provide for gardens. Since small trees naturally yield less brushwood, the Lala find themselves driven to cut still larger areas of woodland, being caught thus in a vicious circle of increasing demands upon the land and decreasing adequacy of the land to meet those demands.[22]

Can we now discern any resource practices in the *citemene* complex which are so clearly within the set of gainful processes as to contradict the universally quantified proposition that every resource complex falls within the set of nongainful processes? For the present, we shall only consider this proposition as a description of what *is*, rather than as a description of what *could be*. Can we, then, discern any innovations, adaptations, and experiments in *citemene* agriculture which represent a trend toward greater efficiency in combining available factors of production?

A glance at the history of the Bemba- and Lala-related tribes is instructive on the point. All of these peoples share a common origin in the Congo, from which area they have been emigrating over a period of some two centuries. Throughout their recent history, these peoples have shown a readiness to adopt new crops, to prepare their gardens in new ways, and to experiment with new types of *citemene* gardens.[23] The Bemba themselves seem to have been hoe cultivators prior to their migration from the Congo and to have adopted *citemene* agriculture only upon reaching their present site.[24] Today, the Bemba practice of stacking branches in single piles rather than in many small piles is diffusing southward, slowly displacing the southern practice with its heavy border wastage and its inordinate demands upon the woodland. The Bisa people, for instance, who live immediately south of the Bemba, are tending to enlarge their garden beds and are even adopting the Bemba practice of planting old millet gardens to subsequent crop sequences, thus gaining added productivity from their cleared land.[25] Some of the Lala, confronted with a severe shortage of land, have increased their dependence upon kaffir corn, which they plant in mounds rather than in *citemene* clearings.[26] In this way they have increased the productivity of their scarce land, though at the expense of the added labor involved in hoeing up mounds. Another Lala group, whose reserve lands had just been enlarged by governmental action, reverted from kaffir corn back to millet, thereby substituting land for labor.[27]

Generally speaking, tribes whose population is pressing hard upon available resources will reduce the amount of time allowed for forest regrowth, will cut down immature trees, and will destroy ever larger areas of woodland (to compensate for the smaller branches yielded by young trees).[28] Likewise, confronted with choosing between scrubby forest regrowth (which is easily accessible) and well regenerated woodland (which is available only in remote, hilly, or animal-infested areas), most tribes will select the former.[29] In all of these adaptations and experiments, there is an evident capacity on the part of the people to recombine productive factors in ways that will increase their economic efficiency. As woodland becomes an increasingly limiting factor in *citemene* agriculture, new resource practices are devised which economize on woodland—usually the exaction of additional labor. Some tribes in northeastern Rhodesia have even gone so far as to abandon their *citemene* practices, driven to this length by the utter depletion of their woodlands. The Mambwe, for instance, have resorted almost entirely to mounds for their gardens. Also, they have evolved a characteristic four- or five-year crop sequence, at the close of which the land is allowed to rest. Then, after two or three more years, the soil is again dug up into mounds and the sequence is resumed. The Mambwe have in this way developed a semi-permanent agricultural complex. Similar adaptations and experiments are under way elsewhere in northeastern Rhodesia.[30]

The Range and Limits of a Resource Complex

If, then, we are to consider as "gainful" those resource practices which are efficient in realizing culturally defined sustenance needs, we can hardly deny that the term fits some elements of the *citemene* complex. The peoples of northeastern Rhodesia do combine and recombine productive factors with a view to increasing the net returns on their capital and labor—or, more accurately, with a view to maintaining existing total returns in the face of declining supplies of productive factors. As woodland becomes depleted, for instance, they tend to substitute units of labor for units of capital, e.g., by hoeing up old millet gardens into mounds, thereby prolonging the productivity of their cleared land. Such adaptive practices clearly falsify the universal truth of the proposition that all elements of an existing resource complex fall outside the set of gainful processes. In at least one case, that of northeastern Rhodesia, there is a resource complex which includes some practices that lie within the set of gainful practices.

Before considering the full significance of this finding, let us turn to the other of our two hypotheses, the one which asserts that, in any social order, the elements of a resource complex must lie wholly inside the set of gainful resource processes. Are any practices within the *citemene* complex so clearly nongainful as to refute the universal truth of this hypothesis? As before, we shall consider this hypothesis for the present as a description of what *is*, rather than as a description of what *could be*. Specifically, then, are there any survivals, anomalies, or contradictions which are so low on a scale of efficiency as to clearly exemplify practices lying outside the set of gainful resource processes?

A natural approach to this question will be to look for tribes whose resource practices are imperfectly suited to their habitats. Over the whole of Northern Rhodesia are some seventy tribes, most of which have had recent histories of migration.[31] In the course of their continual shifting and moving about there has been considerable borrowing and adopting of new practices. At the same time, however, a number of geographical anomalies have appeared with respect to existing man-land relationships. Tribes which have been displaced from one habitat to another have often retained practices that are not well suited to their new environments. This has given rise to geographically anomalous distributions of resource practices which can only be understood by reference to the particular migration histories of the tribes concerned. For example, where the Bangweulu country of northeastern Rhodesia now supports a population of some 200 persons per square mile, an ecologically equivalent habitat in the nearby Chambezi basin remains quite undeveloped for want of occupants that are culturally equipped to exploit it.[32] Crop distributions likewise show geographical anomalies. The satisfactory cultivation of kaffir corn, for instance, calls for more fertile soil and more labor than does the cultivation of finger millet. Most tribes in northeastern Rhodesia grow some of both crops, but the proportions in which they are grown vary from tribe to tribe as much with tribal custom as with soil conditions.[33] So too, the practice of mounding is found associated with finger millet in some tribes, kaffir corn in other tribes, and root crops in still other tribes—often quite irrespective of soil, climate, and other physical factors. Such variations are to be ascribed to past migrations which have disrupted previous man-land relationships. Practices that may have been fairly efficient in a previous habitat have survived as anachronisms in a new and different habitat.

The Range and Limits of a Resource Complex

There is yet another type of survival which figures in the *citemene* complex. This has to do with the mode of organization of *citemene* practices. Several of the tribes of northeastern Rhodesia, notably the Bemba, Lala, Lamba, Kaonde, Lunda, and Bisa possess broadly similar cultures: their languages are related; they all observe matrilineal descent and inheritance; and in all of them residence is generally in the wife's village.[34] These features of social organization impose certain limits to the efficiency of *citemene* practices, however necessary those features may be to sustaining the complex as a whole. They limit people's capacity to respond to new incentives and they impede the free substitution of productive factors which is so essential to improving productive efficiency.

The operation of these limiting factors can be seen in Bemba economic organization. One of the important units of productive enterprise among the Bemba is the group consisting of a man and his sons-in-law.[35] Sons-in-law are expected, upon their betrothal, to take up residence in the village of their wives. There they incur certain traditional obligations to their father-in-law, consisting principally of labor at cutting trees, hoeing, and garden preparation. It is, therefore, the number of daughters which a man has, and the industriousness of their respective husbands, which determines his economic position. The factor combinations which are thus given to a household enterprise by its procreative and marital circumstances are not susceptible of rational manipulation; a man cannot buy daughters, and he cannot sell incompetent sons-in-law! [36] Such fixities in factor combinations set obvious limits to the efficiency of Bemba resource practices.

Other features of Bemba social organization likewise

limit the efficiency of *citemene* practices. Individuals, for example, who desire the help of friends in some arduous project at tree cutting or mounding will often give a party. The quantity of food and beer consumed at such parties is generally out of proportion to the amount of work accomplished, though for some individuals (e.g., widows), it is the only way of getting the work done at all.[37] Contradictions of this kind are of course ubiquitous to folk cultures the world over. They are doubtless "functional" too, in the sense that they motivate individuals to do certain things that might not otherwise get done at all. At the same time, though, they inevitably thwart the attainment of a least-cost combination of productive factors. Resource practices result whose efficiency puts them outside the set of gainful practices.

The existence of such practices would seem to falsify the universal truth of the proposition that all elements of an existing resource complex lie within the set of gainful resource processes. The *citemene* complex of northeastern Rhodesia affords clear instances of resource practices which are low enough on a scale of efficiency (however necessary they may be on psychological grounds) to be unmistakably nongainful. Maximal efficiency is not a necessary attribute of every element of a going resource complex.

The two hypotheses which have been at issue in this chapter, then, would appear to be unacceptable as universally quantified propositions, at least so far as actually existing resource complexes are concerned. In contradiction to these hypotheses, the elements of a resource complex may lie on both sides of a boundary between the gainful and the nongainful. In the case of *citemene* agriculture, some practices are gainful and some are nongainful; both coexist as components of the *citemene* complex.

The Range and Limits of a Resource Complex

To close the matter with this observation, however, would still leave the two foregoing hypotheses ostensibly descriptive of a resource complex as it *might be*. In this interpretation, of course, both hypotheses become conjectures which no amount of empirical data could confirm or refute. Yet, they are plausible statements which deserve to be evaluated as to their truth or falsity. The issue thus presented concerns the range of variability of an existing resource complex. What are the limits of variations which attach to a resource complex?

We can approach this question by a further analysis of *citemene* agriculture, this time in terms of the dual problem: What *might* this complex be and what *might not* it be? What changes could the complex withstand and still be recognizable as *citemene* agriculture? Throughout this study we have assumed that changes in a resource complex involve more than a simple addition or subtraction of resource processes. There are interdependencies in the set of practices which comprise a resource complex such that some elements cannot be added to or subtracted from the whole without destroying those interdependencies and therewith the complex itself.

Our analysis of *citemene* agriculture has already indicated quite a variety of practices that comport with a viable resource complex. Techniques of tree cutting, methods of stacking brushwood, particular crop sequences, and proportions among crops, all vary from tribe to tribe and from village to village. Yet the same *citemene* complex is recognizable throughout these variations. What, then, are the limits beyond which changes could not be made without destroying the complex itself?

The reality of such limits becomes apparent upon consideration of the industrial transformation which has followed upon the opening of the famous copperbelt in Northern Rhodesia.[38] After a somewhat irregular development in the 1930s, copper mining in Northern Rhodesia experienced a rapid expansion which, by 1949, placed the country in third place among the world's copper producers.[39] This development has given rise to a labor force of some 45,000 wage earners who are directly engaged in mining and quarrying, as well as another 130,000 wage earners who are employed in manufacturing, construction, transportation, commerce, etc.[40]

Where do these wage earners come from? By far the greater number of them are men who have left their tribes for briefer or lengthier periods of industrial employment. Over half have left their families behind in their home villages.[41] Most of these industrial workers are young men who make frequent visits back to their home villages but return permanently only in their late middle age. From the standpoint of the rural economy, of course, these absentee men represent a critical loss of labor power. In the Bemba tribe, 41 per cent of the men are at work on the copperbelt.[42] Among the Lala, 44 per cent are away at work.[43] Whole villages have been left occupied mainly by women, children, older men, and a few wage earners who happen to be temporarily at home visiting their families.

Such a redeployment of the labor force has had a profound effect upon agriculture in Northern Rhodesia. Male labor of course is indispensable to certain phases of *citemene* farming. Such practices as tree cutting, garden fencing, and mounding are arduous tasks which can only be done by able bodied men.[44] With so many of a village's men away at the mines, these tasks are no longer being adequately performed, and agricultural output has declined. Food shortages and hunger have been the most immediate results. Villagers have attempted to minimize the decline in their agricultural output by recombining productive factors in various ways. Instead of making new clearings in the woodland every year, they have continued working old millet gardens until the soil has become utterly exhausted.[45] When new clearings are necessary, the trees are simply chopped down rather than pollarded. This technique is dictated by the physical limitations of the older men who remain in the villages. It has the effect, unfortunately, of so obliterating the trees that they cannot regenerate. Scrub growth and grassland are thus succeeding forest growth in parts of Northern Rhodesia, and soil which was already poor is deteriorating even further.[46] Many of the skills involved in *citemene* farming are also being lost as young men, instead of joining their father-in-laws at agricultural production, leave the village for wage work on the copperbelt.

These recent changes in *citemene* agriculture seem to be of a different order of magnitude than those which attended past migrations of people in this part of Africa. New processes have obviously been added to the complement of practices comprising *citemene* agriculture. Likewise, some older practices have been discontinued. These changes represent new combinations of productive factors. But they represent more than just that; they entail a breakdown of the *citemene* complex itself. Certain interdependencies among the original practices comprising the complex have been disrupted, and with them has gone the very capacity of the complex to maintain itself.

The nature of these interdependencies is brought to light

by the change which has taken place in people's economic motivation. Among the Bemba, to illustrate from a single tribe, a traditional respect attaches to the authority and influence of tribal chiefs—particularly to that of the paramount chief. This respect for the authority of a chief figures prominently in people's motivation to work. To be sure, any man wants to make as large a millet garden as he can, so as to provide food for his family. But he does not particularly desire a surplus of food over his immediately foreseeable needs, nor does he value hard work for its own sake. Surplus food is likely to be construed as evidence of witchcraft, and hard work by itself is accorded little social approval. The will to produce, then, stems not so much from these considerations as from the Bemba's belief that their chief is able to intervene in the control that ancestral spirits have over their gardens. The chief's prayers to ancestral spirits are considered determinative of every man's and every village's economic fortunes. Moreover, it is the chief who at least nominally dispenses residence rights to each individual, feeds destitute persons, and manages tribal affairs. He, in return, expects deference, tribute, and labor service.[47] A Bemba who fails in his duties to his chief, or who neglects certain ritual activities, might so alienate the ancestral spirits that they would withhold their favor from him. This, the Bemba believe, could lead to an accident while cutting trees, to destruction of gardens by wild animals, or to a failure of the land to yield crops, etc.[48]

Along with the respect which traditionally attaches to the Bemba chief, there is a desire on the part of chiefs and commoners alike to surround one's self with a group of followers—people who will live near one, move to another village when one moves, help one at agricultural chores and generally serve as evidence of one's personal importance. Such a following can be secured by various means: having several daughters who, upon betrothal, will bring additional labor (sons-in-law); earning a reputation for being able to provide others with economic security; and having the political skill with which to head off contention among one's followers and to win favor from one's own chief. This desire for a following has been an important economic incentive for ambitious Bemba.

To an increasing extent, however, wage employment on the copperbelt has undercut these traditional economic incentives. Most immediately, it has provided young men with an alternative to working for their fathers-in-law. Instead of cutting trees and making gardens, a young man can send cash to his father-in-law. Supposedly this money is to be spent for hiring men to do the garden work, but it is more often spent for consumer's goods, with the result that less gardening is done and less food is produced. When a man does return to his father-in-law's village, he is likely to work indifferently or not at all. Particularly onerous chores, such as hoeing up mounds—a practice which is indispensable to the cultivation of certain crops—tend to be avoided by the young men or are done carelessly.[49] The traditional work group consisting of a number of men and their common father-in-law is no longer capable of providing the incentives and sanctions that would ensure productive activity on the part of its members.[50]

The availability of wage employment outside the tribal economy has tended, too, to weaken the respect of younger men for their elders.[51] In the past, this respect had a firm basis in the mutual dependence which obtained within the household enterprise and within the larger tribal system. Now that individuals can unilaterally withdraw from the system and still survive, the sanctions which previously operated to maintain respect for elders have been nullified. With this has gone much of the point to surrounding one's self with a group of followers. With it, too, has gone the ability of village headmen and chiefs to ensure the economic security of their followers and to carry on tribal affairs. Individuals no longer make their proper contributions of labor and tribute to their chiefs, with the result that the latter lack the wherewithal to fulfil their traditional obligations.[52] The respect which has traditionally attached to chiefly authority has thus weakened to the point that it no longer dominates the economic motivation of Bemba individuals.[53] Young men are skeptical of their chief's religious powers; they ridicule their elders' rituals; and indeed they show a disdain for productive activity generally.[54] In the meantime, the output of food has declined, the soil is overcropped, the trees are mercilessly chopped down, and the entire *citemene* complex is disintegrating. The complex is no longer capable of imposing a constraint or necessity upon its human agents such that there will be willing conformity to the practices which constitute it.

Here we seem to have the distinguishing feature of a viable set of resource practices: its capacity to motivate its human agents to willingly perform the practices which comprise it. And it is this willing conformity on the part of human agents which transforms a mere aggregate of resource processes into a resource complex. The interdependencies or invariance properties of a resource complex derive from this relationship of constraint or necessity which obtains between its human agents and its component practices. Viability thus becomes the *differentia specifica* of a resource complex.

Every resource complex, it would appear, has a range of variability within which new practices can be readily added and old ones readily subtracted. The known history of *citemene* agriculture reveals a number of such changes in specific practices, all of which comported with the viability of the system. But with the industrialization of Northern Rhodesia, the *citemene* complex has encountered a limit to its range of variation. It is apparently unable to incorporate industrial wage employment into its complement of resource practices. A break point has thus been reached, a point marked by the dissolution of the relationship of constraint or necessity which had previously obtained between resource users and their resource practices. *Citemene* processes are still observed in northeastern Rhodesia but they no longer have the essential features of a resource complex.

These facts put a new light on the problem which has been engaging us in this chapter. Whether *citemene* agriculture, or any other resource complex, could or could not be reorganized so that all its elements were on one side or the other of a boundary between the gainful and the nongainful is, on empirical grounds, an unanswerable question. What *is* clear, however, is the fact that the new resource processes which are developing in northeastern Rhodesia occupy positions on a "scale" of value which are quite incomparable to those occupied by *citemene* practices. They are so different that it is pointless to seek any single cutting point between the gainful and the nongainful that will be applicable both to the old and the new resource processes of northeastern Rhodesia. As Richards has observed, ". . . the introduction of British rule, money, and European goods has cut completely across old economic objectives. . . ." [55] Many individuals have turned to cash crop farming or to grazing. Thousands of men have found in industrial wage employment a more or less permanent source of livelihood. These people are participating in a set of resource processes that lie outside the *citemene* complex. Policy measures aimed at encouraging such developments should be recognized for what they are: actions which effect a change to an altogether different resource system. The possible future success of such measures cannot be taken as confirmation of the hypothesis that any resource complex is capable of reorganization so that all its elements lie wholly within one or the other of the sets of gainful or nongainful resource processes. That hypothesis remains a pure conjecture. So far as evidence concerning *citemene* agriculture is instructive on the point, changes in the elements of a resource complex beyond a critical break point represent a transition to a new and different resource system.

We must conclude, then, that the social orders of northeastern Rhodesia afford no confirmation of either of the two contrary hypothesis, viz., that: (a) every element of a resource complex lies outside the set of gainful resource processes; and (b) every element of a resource complex lies inside the set of gainful resource processes. Indeed, these social orders falsify the two hypotheses so far as the latter are supposedly descriptive of all existing resource complexes. There remains only the hypothesis that a resource complex can include elements both from the set of gainful practices and from the set of nongainful practices. This, of course, is a tautologically true proposition—one whose truth would call for no empirical confirmation anyway. As such, it would not exclude instances of social orders which might conform to one or the other of the two hypotheses whose universal truth we have falsified. By itself, moreover, the proposition allows the inference that the elements of any resource complex are indifferently gainful or nongainful. Manifestly there is no guide to resource policy formation in a "theory" of this kind.

As a matter of fact, our entire discussion up to this point has rendered progressively indeterminate the formal location of a resource complex with respect to the sets of possible, adoptable, and gainful resource processes. In Chapter III we were driven to the conclusion that there could be no generalized rationale for policy efforts which were aimed at locating a resource complex at the three coinciding optima of these sets—the possible, the adoptable, and the gainful— for the reason that such a coincidence does not universally hold for all social orders. In the present chapter, we have been compelled to recognize that there could be no generalized rationale for policy efforts that were designed, in effect at least, to so improve or reduce the efficiency of a people's resource practices that those practices would lie wholly within the set of gainful processes or wholly within the set of nongainful processes—again for the reason that neither of these relationships universally holds for all social orders.

Are we to conclude then that there is no determinacy in the location of a resource complex with respect to the possible, the adoptable, and the gainful sets of resource processes? Must we forego our search for an objective guide to the formulation of rational resource plans and policies? Or can we, by considering further the criterion of viability which has been advanced in this chapter, arrive at a positive formulation of the relationship which a resource complex bears to its environing universe of possible, adoptable, and gainful resource processes and their respective complements? Let us take a closer look at this criterion of viability, according to which it is the willing conformity of resource users to their practices which constitutes a resource complex.

NOTES

1. Paul B. Sears, *This Is Our World* (Norman, Okla.: University of Oklahoma Press, 1937), p. 247.

2. Jacks, in G. V. Jacks and R. O. Whyte, *Vanishing Lands* (New York: Doubleday, Doran and Co., Inc., 1939), chaps. xx-xxi.

3. Kenneth Boulding, in William L. Thomas, Jr. (ed.), *Man's Role in Changing the Face of the Earth* (Chicago: University of Chicago Press, 1956), p. 432.

4. C. G. Trapnell and J. N. Clothier, *The Soils, Vegetation and Agricultural Systems of North Western Rhodesia: Report of the Ecological Survey* (Lusaka: The Government Printer, 1937); C. G. Trapnell, *The Soils, Vegetation and Agriculture of North-Eastern Rhodesia: Report of the Ecological Survey* (Lusaka: The Government Printer, 1943); Audrey I. Richards, *Land, Labour and Diet in Northern Rhodesia* (London: Oxford University Press, for International African Institute, 1939); Wilfred Whitely, *Bemba and Related Peoples of Northern Rhodesia* (London: International African Institute, 1950); William Allan, *Studies in African Land Usage in Northern Rhodesia* ("Rhodes-Livingstone Papers" No. 15 [London: Rhodes-Livingstone Institute, 1949]); D. U. Peters, *Land Usage in Serenje District* ("Rhodes-Livingstone Papers" No. 19 [London: Rhodes-Livingstone Institute, 1950]).

5. Pierre Gourou, *The Tropical World* (New York: Longmans, Green and Co. Ltd., 1953), p. 25.

6. Trapnell, *op. cit.*, p. 16.

7. Peters, *op. cit.*, p. xvi.
8. *Ibid.*, pp. 68-69.
9. Gourou, *op. cit.*, p. 26; Trapnell and Clothier, *op. cit.*, p. 58.
10. Richards, *op. cit.*, p. 185.
11. *Ibid.*, pp. 352-62.
12. *Ibid.*, pp. 300-1.
13. *Ibid.*, pp. 289, 292.
14. Whiteley, *op. cit.*, pp. 10-11.
15. Richards, *op. cit.*, pp. 296-97; Trapnell, *op. cit.*, pp. 37-38.
16. Richards, *op. cit.*, p. 299.
17. *Ibid.*, pp. 316-17.
18. *Ibid.*, pp. 288, 302-5; Trapnell, *op. cit.*, p. 40.
19. Trapnell, *op. cit.*, p. 29; Whiteley, *op. cit.*, p. 35.
20. Peters, *op. cit.*, pp. 33-36; Trapnell, *op. cit.*, p. 78.
21. Trapnell, *op. cit.*, p. 78.
22. Peters, *op. cit.*, pp. xiii-xiv, 27.
23. Richards, *op. cit.*, 229-30.
24. Trapnell, *op. cit.*, p. 33.
25. *Ibid.*, p. 79.
26. Allan, *op. cit.*, p. 53.
27. *Ibid.*, pp. 61, 69.
28. Peters, *op. cit.*, p. xiv.
29. *Ibid.*, pp. 48-49.
30. Trapnell, *op. cit.*, pp. 36, 41-42, 81.
31. Lord Hailey, *An African Survey* (London: Oxford University Press), p. 452.
32. Trapnell, *op. cit.*, p. 25.
33. *Ibid.*, p. 77.
34. Richards, *op. cit.*, pp. 16-17; Whiteley, *op. cit.*, pp. 1-5.
35. Richards, *op. cit.*, pp. 112-14, 383.
36. Cf. *ibid.*, pp. 172-75.
37. Richards, *op. cit.*, p. 146.
38. Hailey, *op. cit.*, pp. 1387-88.
39. *Review of Economic Conditions in Africa* (New York: United Nations, Department of Economic Affairs, 1951), p. 47.
40. *Review of Economic Activity in Africa, 1950 to 1954* ("Supplement to the World Economic Report, 1953-4" [New York: United Nations, Department of Economic and Social Affairs, 1955]), Appendix, Table E. Data are for 1952.
41. Daryll Forde, "Social Aspects of Urbanization and Industrialization in Africa: a General Review," in *Social Implications of Industrialization and Urbanization in Africa South of the Sahara* ("Tensions and Technology Series" No. 5 [New York: UNESCO, 1956]), pp. 31-32.

42. Whiteley, *op. cit.*, p. 22, fn. 1.
43. Peters, *op. cit.*, p. xv.
44. Godfrey Wilson, *An Essay on the Economics of Detribalization in Northern Rhodesia, Part I* ("Rhodes-Livingstone Papers" No. 5 [Livingstone, Northern Rhodesia: The Rhodes-Livingstone Institute, 1941]), p. 51.
45. Allan, *op. cit.*, p. 36.
46. Hailey, *op. cit.*, p. 1088.
47. Richards, *op. cit.*, pp. 266ff.
48. *Ibid.*, pp. 23-24, 234-35.
49. *Ibid.*, pp. 304, 309.
50. *Ibid.*, p. 133.
51. *Ibid.*, p. 372.
52. *Ibid.*, p. 263.
53. *Ibid.*, p. 403.
54. *Ibid.*, pp. 372, 380.
55. *Ibid.*, p. 216.

CHAPTER V

THE SOCIAL STATICS
OF A RESOURCE COMPLEX

All concord's born of contraries.
BEN JONSON

WE ARE STILL in quest of a theory which will tell us what kinds of processes universally characterize a resource complex. Our object is to provide the planner and policy maker with a generalized rationale for making and justifying decisions that would change or maintain particular resource practices.

Up to this point we have established only two propositions, and both are negative. We have shown that: (1) It is not the case that in every social order there is a coincidence of the ecologically, ethnologically, and economically optimum resource processes; and (2) It is not the case that in every social order a resource complex will lie exclusively on one side or the other of a plausible division between gainful and nongainful practices. Can we, now, go further and formulate some positive propositions which will have some degree of credibility?

At the end of our last chapter, we decided to take a closer look at the assumption that it is the willing conformity of resource users to their practices which constitutes a resource complex. This concept of *willing conformity* immediately raises a host of philosophical problems, all bound up with the related notions of necessity, obligation, freedom, and the like. For our purposes, however, it should be sufficient to note that a person's conformity to a set of resource practices implies some latent inclination on his part to do otherwise —otherwise, it would be tautological to speak of his conduct as "conforming."

Conformity, that is to say, involves a certain ambivalence on the part of a resource user with respect to a set of adoptable resource processes. On the one hand, there are incentives for every user to employ processes that are clearly gainful to him with respect to their economic efficiency. On the other hand, there are other incentives, no less real, which lead him to accept bounds to his preference for gainful processes. The interpretation of this ambivalence is a task that is going to occupy us throughout much of the remainder of this study. For the present, however, it is enough to note that the existence of such a psychological property as ambivalence, with respect to the choice of gainful resource practices, carries with it an interesting implication. If every resource user is indeed attracted to gainful processes, and is at the same time deterred from *some* of those gainful processes, it would appear that a population of resource users will find itself committed to some gainful practices and to some nongainful practices. Such a population, in short, will have a resource complex which includes elements from both the gainful and the nongainful sets of resource processes. This proposition, if it can be empirically sustained, is a good deal more specific than the negative finding of our previous chapter, viz., that a resource complex may not lie wholly within the set of gainful processes or wholly within the set of nongainful processes. The present proposition would imply that a resource complex *must* lie athwart both the gainful and the nongainful, thereby including practices that differ widely in their productive efficiency. In this event, the location of a resource complex within the universe of the possible, the adoptable, and the gainful (with their respective complements) would be considerably more determinate than has so far appeared to be the case.

These considerations call for empirical demonstration. Since our present hypothesis is a positive, rather than a negative one, we are going to follow a somewhat different approach from the one employed in our previous examples. Rather than refuting a hypothesis by adducing a single deviant case, we shall attempt to support our hypothesis by adducing a single conforming case. Obviously, this will be no proof at all. It will be a method of illustration, and nothing more. Fortunately, in Chapter IX the same hypothesis is to be subjected to stricter canons of proof, and its credibility will be somewhat enhanced. For the present, we shall be primarily interested in a case which will serve two purposes: first, that of illustrating the proposition that there is an ambivalent disposition on the part of resource users, stemming from the constitution of every social order, which commits them to a set of practices that includes elements from both the gainful and the nongainful; second, that of illustrating another, but corollary proposition, that the composition of a resource complex changes over time as exogenous factors provide an occasion for previously inhibited propensities, or incentives, to realize themselves, ultimately reaching a limit beyond which it becomes an altogether different entity, a resource congeries.

To serve such a dual purpose, the case which we select should be historical in nature, affording a sufficient time span over which we can observe both the static and the dynamic features of the resource complex in question. The example which we have chosen is the open field farming complex of the medieval English Midlands, a system more idiomatically known as "champion husbandry." This is a resource complex which has probably been more thoroughly described and analyzed than any other single resource complex in the world, owing in large part to the abundance of documentary materials for every phase of its existence. Moreover, it is a case about which a substantial consensus of scholarly opinion has been achieved as the result of a long process of critical historical research. We should be hard put indeed to find a more fully documented case that would answer so well to our immediate theoretical problem.

Accordingly, for the empirical materials in this and the succeeding chapter we shall turn to the English open field farming complex. In the present chapter, we shall be primarily interested in the social statics of this resource complex, taking particular note of the ambivalent disposition which is engendered in resource users by their social order and the dual commitment which they consequently exhibit to both gainful and nongainful practices. In the following chapter we shall trace the decline of the open field complex and its transition to another, rather different kind of resource system, relating this trend to exogenous forces which permitted a release of previously inhibited psychological incentives *pari passu* with changes in the social order.

Open field farming, or champion husbandry, is the English variant of a resource complex that flourished throughout the lowlands of Western Europe for some one thousand years. In England, it was the principal form of agriculture in the Midlands between 500 and 1500, reaching its fullest development in the thirteenth century.[1] The outstanding feature of the complex was its apportionment of a community's arable land into two or three large fields, each of which was alternately tilled and fallowed over a two or three year cycle. The effect of this arrangement was a stable proportion between tilled and fallow land from one year to the next.[2] To appreciate the importance—indeed the necessity, for its time—of this arrangement, we shall have to consider some additional features of the open field resource complex.

The English Midlands are characterized by a heavy, clayey soil which in its original climax state was dominated by oak and ash forests. Not until the Saxon conquests were these forests cleared and put to the plow. The land which was thus opened to cultivation had a soil structure rather typical of humid forested regions, where the layer of humus is generally underlain by a layer of highly acid mineral soil. Cultivation of such land requires mixing the two layers into a granular soil structure.[3] For this purpose, the heavy moldboard plow, drawn by a team of oxen or horses, is ideally suited. The weight and the power of such a plow, drawn by six or eight animals, gives the depth of plowing which is necessary to till soils of this kind.

Any resource complex which involves the use of animal drawn equipment will immediately confront a practical problem: that of providing feed for the beasts. In medieval England, the problem was all the greater in that farmers were ignorant of grass seed and hence were unable to provide their animals with sown fodder.[4] Their only recourse was to set aside part of their arable land as pasture. This they did in two ways: first, by reserving limited portions of low, moist land for meadow, and second, by dividing most of their arable land into large fields, either two or three in number, and rotating these as between cultivation and pasturage. It is this second feature which is most distinctive of the open field resource complex—a feature that was dictated by the necessity of providing feed for the animals who furnished power for the plows.[5]

An abiding dilemma presently confronted the medieval English farmer: any increase in the amount of land that he might put to crops would mean a decrease in the amount of land that he could put to pasture. The ultimate limit to such expansion of cropland was the necessity of maintaining sufficient land in pasture to support the oxen and horses of the community. Hence, as population growth gradually forced cropland to expand, oxen in particular became a crucial limiting factor in open field resource practices.[6] A second important limiting factor was the supply of plows. Owing to a pervasive capital insufficiency in the medieval economy, plows were never numerous enough to permit their widespread ownership among the individual members of a community. This shortage of both plows and oxen ac-

[86]

counts for an interesting feature of the open field resource complex—the practice of communal plowing. Since no one peasant could expect to own, by himself, a plow and eight oxen, each man would simply pool such of these as he had with the contributions of other peasants, forming with them a co-operative plow team.[7]

Open field farming was thus carried out by small groups of peasants who had pooled their short supplies of animals, plows, and labor and who together tilled one or two well defined fields (out of the community's total of two or three fields), leaving the remaining field fallow and pasturing their beasts upon it. Year by year the community would rotate these fields so that each one of them would be rested during the second or third year.

Within this arrangement of fields lay the holdings of the individual peasants. Each man's holding consisted of a collection of long, narrow strips of land scattered about in the cultivated field or fields. The elongated nature of these strips is related to the fact that less turnabout walking is entailed for animals when land is plowed in long, narrow rectangles than when it is plowed in more or less equilateral rectangles.[8] The apportionment of land within an open field was related to the composition of the plow team and to the day-by-day sequence of plowing. Thus, the owner of the plow might receive the first portion of plowed land, the owner of the leading pair of oxen might receive the next portion, the owner of another ox or two would receive another portion, etc., with the shares being proportional to the contribution which each man had made to the plow team. The entire series would then be repeated in plowing the next block of land, with the relative position of each individual's portion being the same as it had been on the land previously plowed.[9] The significance of this intermixed arrangement of holdings for people's attitudes toward gainful and nongainful practices will be considered shortly. For the present, it is enough to be cognizant of the co-operative nature of plowing in the open field resource complex and the intermixed arrangement of the scattered land holdings of plow team members in such a complex.

The annual sequence of practices within this arrangement of holdings and fields can be viewed as a function partly of medieval agricultural technology and partly of the seasonal variations and growth characteristics of the crops which were grown. Plow agriculture naturally lends itself to the cultivation of small grains rather than root crops. In medieval England the principal grains were rye, barley, oats and wheat.[10] A field which had lain fallow for a year would be given two or three summer plowings to destroy weed growth, and then, in the autumn, would be sown to rye or wheat. For the harvest, sickles or scythes, wielded by bands of five men or women, were employed to cut the stalks. Following harvest a field would be opened to cattle that would feed on its stubble; the residue was then plowed in or burned.[11] In a two-field rotation, the remaining field would lay fallow, providing pasture for the community's animals. In a three-field rotation one of the remaining fields, after the previous year's wheat stubble had been plowed in, would be sown during the spring with oats and barley, while the other field lay fallow.[12] From one year to the next the fields would be rotated, thus ensuring a rest to the land once every two or three years. In the scarce and valuable meadow land, grass would be mowed for hay, after which it, too, was opened to grazing. Surrounding waste lands provided additional grazing for a community's animals as well as materials for building purposes.[13]

Our interest in these details of open field agriculture lies primarily in the relationship which obtained between the medieval resource user and his resource complex. How did the medieval English farmer experience his resource complex? What spontaneity and what constraint are manifest in his observance of its component practices? In what sense did he willingly conform his behavior to those practices? Of course the outstanding feature of open field agriculture was its co-operative character. This is apparent in the apportionment of a community's land into fields that were tilled and fallowed in rotation with each other, such that concerted, uniform behavior by all members of that community was imperative in regard to the choice of cropland and the pasturing of animals. It is further apparent in the intermixed distribution of individual land holdings, itself a consequence of the co-operative character of the plow teams, by virtue of which the choice of crops, the time for plowing and sowing, and the plan of harvesting, all had to be done uniformly and in concert by the various members of the community.

Open field agriculture, then, was a resource complex which required a high degree of conformity on the part of its human agents to the practices which comprised it. The sanctions for this conformity lay ultimately with the community, operating either through informal face-to-face relationships or through formal judicial proceedings. In either event, conformity was enforceable by community action. The outcome was a set of resource practices whose observance by every member of the community had a high degree of likelihood, both in fact and in the anticipations which each person had of his fellows. It is not surprising, then, that open field agriculture should have become a rather rigid, stereotyped set of resource practices whose structure was invariant relative to changes outside the complex. In our next chapter we shall discover that this invariance had its limit, so that when exogenous changes eventually reached a critical magnitude, the entire complex broke down. So long, however, as a fundamental stability obtained among the structural parameters of the complex, there was little scope for individual variation in the time or manner of plowing, sowing, reaping, pasturing, etc.[14] The individual peasant had indeed to be a conformist, either willing or unwilling.

Yet the medieval English farmer was by no means blind to opportunities for personal gain. Now and then an individual would employ resource processes which exceeded the bounds of his resource complex. Some of these nonconforming activities were plainly delinquent: pasturing too many animals on fallow or waste land; putting one's animals in a tilled field before harvest; not mowing at the proper time; plowing into the fallow field or into one's neighbor's holding; harvesting grain ahead of time; etc.[15] Such offenses were ubiquitous phenomena in every open field community and they had to be inhibited by appropriate repressive measures. Yet their recurrence testifies to the capacity of the individual resource user, no matter how well imbued he might be with the established practices of his resource complex, to perceive alternative processes that might better serve his immediate advantage.[16]

The Social Statics of a Resource Complex

There were, however, other nonconforming processes that were not so clearly delinquent, and which further demonstrate an awareness by the medieval resource user of processes alternative to those which comprised his resource complex. The use of the scythe is a case in point. Originally employed only for harvesting hay, the scythe became increasingly popular for harvesting grain, gradually superseding the sickle which had previously been used. The advantage of the scythe lay in the saving of labor time which it afforded. However, by cutting stalks closer to the ground, the scythe also reduced the amount of stubble which would remain in a field after harvest and thus reduced the number of animals which a field could carry.[17] A nice economic problem was thus posed: that of economically substituting scythes for oxen. Since in the nature of things, one man's use of the scythe would mean everyone's use of the scythe, the two factors (scythes and oxen) were not continuously substitutable. The gradual adoption of the scythe has, therefore, to be related to other exogenous forces which were affecting the open field resource complex. The fact remains, however, that in this instance, medieval farmers did endeavor to combine productive factors in more efficient proportions, revealing an incentive to seek additional gainful practices beyond those which presently constituted their resource complex.

Such an incentive for gainful resource processes had obviously to be held in check, above all in a resource complex which, like open field agriculture, was so highly co-operative in nature. Conformity to established practices was a minimum condition for the economic security of all. Each individual thus had a stake in the conforming behavior of his

fellows. What he considered to be his rights were the reciprocal of others' duties. Yet for one man to assert that others
had duties implied an acknowledgment that he too had
duties.[18] No one could protest that his neighbor had over-
stocked the fallow field with animals unless he was willing
to hold himself similarly accountable to the community for
the number of animals that he might pasture. The acknowledgment that one had certain duties, when generalized into
a norm for proper conduct, became an incentive to limit
one's preference for gainful processes. The locus of this incentive lay in the individual's moral conscience, but it had
its deeper roots in self interest. Each man's conformity to
open field practices gave warrant to his claim that others,
too, should conform so as to ensure to every member of the
community a dependable (though not a maximum) return
on his productive efforts. It further enabled each individual
to attach some degree of likelihood to the conforming behavior of his fellows (a point whose significance we shall
presently want to elaborate upon).

A fundamental ambivalence thus characterized the medieval resource user with respect to the resource processes
that were technically available to him. The psychological
conflict involved in such ambivalence is particularly apparent in the various kinds of surreptitious activity which
plagued every medieval community: encroachments of one
or two furrows into a neighbor's land, removal of boundary
markers, trespassing, borrowing equipment and animals
without permission, etc. Sometimes, too, there would be
connivance, as in the unauthorized exchanges of land holdings made for the sake of more efficient management, and in
the tacit agreements occasionally made to plow up and till

fallow or waste pasture land. These phenomena reveal a latent inclination on the part of the individual resource user to evade and even violate some of the established practices of his resource complex—an inclination which on occasion would become quite manifest. But the comparative impotence of the single individual, who in the long run obviously had to get along with his fellows, made the inhibition of nonconforming inclinations a more prudent alternative. His very awareness of the likelihood of others' conformity was in itself a constraining factor upon his own behavior, owing to that *"normative Kraft des Faktischen"* which Jellinek saw as figuring in so much of law making.[19] In a trial-and-error fashion, then, the medieval English farmer was continually substituting productive factors up to the limit of social tolerance, seeking at one and the same time the contrary objectives of efficiency in factor combinations and security in his customary rights. Being thus attracted to gainful practices and yet being deterred from many of them, he found himself committed to a range of resource practices that varied considerably in their economic efficiency. He found himself, in other words, conforming of his own free will to a resource complex whose component elements lay both in the set of gainful resource processes and in the set of nongainful resource processes.

This ambivalent disposition on the part of the medieval resource user can be more clearly seen if we examine some specific practices which lay, respectively, within the set of gainful resource processes and within the set of nongainful resource processes. Of course any appraisal of the efficiency of open field practices will be hampered by the fact that we have no historical data on marginal costs and revenues for the productive factors involved. Without such data it is impossible to rank practices on a scale of efficiency. What we can do, however, is to differentiate resource practices according to the degree to which they do or do not permit variable proportions in factor combinations. Then, in the case of practices which admit of a wide range of factor combinations, we can look for tendencies within the resource complex toward more efficient proportions among productive factors. In the case of practices whose factor combinations are more or less fixed, we can look for tendencies that maintain those proportions in the face of more efficient alternatives. These two classes of practices may be designated, respectively, as gainful and nongainful.

We may begin by recalling two practices both of which permitted some substitution of productive factors and which, moreover, exhibited tendencies toward more efficient proportions among those factors. As such they would appear to qualify as gainful practices. They are, first, the use of both oxen and horses as draught animals, and second, the use of both two-field and three-field rotations. Open field agriculture allowed some variation in the proportions with which oxen and horses, and two-field and three-field rotations could be combined.

In the case of oxen and horses, there were economic advantages and disadvantages with each. Oxen were stronger; they required less attendance; they had a cheaper harness; and, most important, their winter feed was more economical.[20] Horses, on the other hand, were faster than oxen and they could do considerably more plowing in a day.[21] The least-cost combination of these factors would consequently vary with the supply of such other factors as manpower, grain, collars, etc. Hence, medieval agriculture required few fixed proportions in regard to animal power: not only could plow teams vary in size, but their composition might vary from all oxen to mixed oxen and horses.

So, too, with the two-field and three-field rotations. These can be viewed as being different combinations of productive factors. In two-field farming, the tilled land might be sown to both spring and autumn grains. Insofar as these different grains were clearly separated into distinct portions of the cultivated land, a three-field system thereby existed.[22] The extent to which a community thus differentiated its tilled land into seasonally specific crops would vary with the supply of other productive factors. The use of horses as draught animals, for instance, required an ample supply of spring oats, which in turn tended to make the three-field rotation a more efficient practice than the two-field rotation. The size of holdings and the fertility of the soil also affected the relative efficiency of the two kinds of rotations.[23] While the two-field rotation tended with time to yield to the three-field rotation, both arrangements co-existed throughout the English Midlands right up to the sixteenth century.

In examples like these, where opportunity existed for variation in the combination of productive factors, there was at least some possibility of reaching a fair degree of efficiency in the practices that would be employed in any given community. While the possibility might not always be seized upon, there was at least no resistance to a community's taking advantage of it. The substitution of oxen and horses, and two-field and three-field rotations, both of which were ubiquitous and unremitting throughout the history of medieval agriculture, can be viewed as a trial and error quest for more efficient proportions among productive factors. At least some of the practices which resulted from these *tâtonnements* may be considered to have been sufficiently high on a scale of efficiency to have fallen within the class of gainful resource practices.

But this was not the case with all open field practices. Some involved factor combinations so fixed that there can be little question of the inefficiency which they sometimes entailed. The origin of this fixity of factor combinations lay in the vested interest which every peasant had in the conforming behavior of his fellows. Consider, for instance, the system of intermixed land holdings wherein each individual's holding consisted of a number of strips of ground scattered about among the tilled fields of a community. This arrangement, as we have seen, was dictated by the co-operative nature of the plow team, not by considerations of efficiency in agricultural production. It was, at least in the first instance, a socially rather than an economically dictated practice—though in the final analysis, it is attributable to the pervasive capital insufficiency of the medieval economy. This intermixed arrangement of land holdings entailed a great deal of waste motion in going from one part of a man's farm to another. It led to encroachments by one neighbor upon the holding of another. Most important, it debarred the imaginative individual from experimenting with new processes. Everyone had to hold to the same schedule of plowing, sowing, cultivating, harvesting, and pasturing because their holdings were so fragmented and intermixed in the open fields of the community.[24]

So, too, the right which every peasant had to pasture his animals in the tilled fields following harvest served as a deterrent to experimentation with new practices. Root crops, such as the turnip, were stubbornly resisted by medieval English peasants in spite of the fact that they would have permitted the feeding of many more animals during the winter months. The reason for this resistance lay in the fact that root crops would mature well after the grain harvest, which was the traditional occasion for turning animals into the fields to graze on the stubble. Adoption of root crops would have destroyed the traditional right which every man had to pasture his animals in the open fields. It is not surprising, then, that these valuable crops could only be introduced into English agriculture after the open field resource complex had pretty well disintegrated.[25]

Another limitation on the substitutability of productive factors in the open field complex was the immobility of land and labor. To understand this fixity, we shall have to consider a feature of the medieval social order that has thus far gone unnoticed. This is the manor. The manor, though varying considerably from one region of England to another in its organizational details, was everywhere an estate that was operated by a feudal lord and cultivated by peasants who had varying degrees of servitude with respect to their lord.[26] The lord of the manor asserted a paramount right over its inhabitants and over their holdings. He also laid claim to some of their labor time or, alternatively, to their money rent. Essentially the manor was an administrative and exploitative arrangement, superimposed upon the peasants' local communities and articulating those communities with the larger social order. Within his manor, the individual peasant had lifetime tenure whether he wanted it or not. His holding, too, was his by the "custom of the manor," so that it could not be freely alienated.[27] Labor and land were thus immobilized by the manorial system. To be sure, some shifting of individuals between tenure statuses took place, and there were occasional leases, exchanges, and loans of land which compromised on the general proscription against alienation.[28] For the most part, however, the manor represented a balance of interests whereby most of its human agents had a stake in the *status quo*. It was, if we may borrow Tawney's apt characterization, a "great collective bargain" between the peasants and their lords.[29] Any serious departure from the "custom of the manor" would have threatened the legitimate expectations of most of its inhabitants and was, as a rule, vigorously resisted.

In these examples, then, we have evidence that there were open field resource practices which involved rather fixed proportions of productive factors. Their efficiency was occasionally less than that of some available alternatives. At certain times and places, they could accordingly be placed in the class of nongainful practices. Many of these practices, despite their inefficiency, were staunchly maintained by their human agents, who saw in their perpetuation a guarantee that customary rights would not be threatened.

The medieval English resource user, we may conclude, was willing to conform to the practices which comprised his open field complex. This willing conformity extended not only to practices which lay within the set of gainful resource processes but also to some which lay within the set of nongainful resource processes—i.e., to practices that varied considerably in their relative productive efficiency. It was this willing conformity of its human agents which endowed open field agriculture with the viability that made it a resource complex—a complex that lasted for some one thousand years before it disintegrated in the face of irresistible changes external to itself.

Before we turn now to an examination of the decline of

open field agriculture let us briefly assess the full import of what has just been said so far as the essential character of a resource complex is concerned. To this end, we shall find it helpful to introduce some notational symbols and to locate these symbols on a schematic diagram of resource processes. The symbols which we shall employ, and their corresponding meanings, are as follows (see Figure 1, reading from left to right):

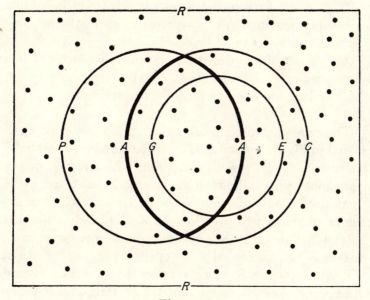

Figure 1.

P,   the set of resource processes which are *possible* in a given organic and physical environment.

A,   the set of resource processes which are *adoptable* by a given population.

G, the set of resource processes which are *gainful* for the members of a given population.

E, the set of resource processes which are *efficient* for the members of a given population.

C, the set of resource processes which are *culturally* available to a given population.

X, the set of resource processes which are included in a resource *system* (the location of which has yet to be determined).

X', the set of resource processes which are included in a resource *complex* (a type of resource system whose location has yet to be determined).

X", the set of resource processes which are included in a resource *congeries* (another type of resource system whose location has yet to be determined).

The relationship of the sets *P, A, G, E* and *C* is represented in Figure 1. Consider, for instance, a particular habitat occupied by a given population. The ecologist or the geographer will not be hard put to specify, in at least hypothetical or conditional terms, the maximum variety of resource processes which will be physically possible for that habitat.[30] This range of physically possible resource processes may be represented as an encircled region *P* situated within a rectangle *R* which represents the whole universe of resource processes, real or fanciful, possible or impossible. The processes themselves may be denoted by dots, such that each dot will correspond to a different combination or proportioning of human and physical factors. Processes which are not possible in a given habitat may be represented by dots lying outside *P* but within *R*.

Within the set *P* of physically possible resource processes we can distinguish between those processes which are adopt-able by the population occupying a given habitat and those which are not adoptable. The ethnologist is able to explain this differentiation in terms of the culture of a people, their history and their contacts with other population groups. The culture of any people will set bounds to the range of resource processes which that people can assimilate or ar-ticulate with their other activities. Those resource processes which are adoptable by the population occupying a given habitat may be represented as a subset A of the set P of pos-sible resource processes. Only adoptable resource processes may be properly considered as comprising the natural re-sources of a people.

This subset A is likewise a subset of set C of socially de-fined activities. By "activities," we have in mind the entire class of processes in which a group of people are conscious agents and in which resource phenomena are in some man-ner involved. The set C is to be identified with what is gen-erally called the "culture" of a people. It may be dia-grammed as an encircled region C situated within the universe of resource processes and overlapping, but not nec-essarily coinciding with, P. This non-coincidence of C and P will represent the fact that not all of the socially defined activities of a people will necessarily be possible in a given habitat. By hypothesis, the subset A of adoptable resource processes will be identical with the overlap, or logical prod-uct, of P and C. In other words, only those resource proc-esses can be adopted which represent socially defined activi-ties as well as organic and physical possibilities. Only such resource processes can be considered as natural resources.

Next, a distinction may be drawn between those adopt-able resource processes which are gainful or advantageous to the individual resource users in some subjective, psychological sense, and those adoptable processes which are not thus gainful. They can be differentiated in terms of productive efficiency. Adoptable processes which lie above any specified cutting point on a scale of productive efficiency will yield a higher magnitude of gainfulness to the individual resource user (in a phenomenal sense of the word) than processes which lie below that point. The former may be represented as a subset G of the set A of adoptable resource processes.

This subset G is also a subset of another more inclusive set E of efficient activities. The set E is comprised of all those production, exchange, and distribution activities of a people which measure up to some formal criteria of efficiency and in which resource phenomena are somehow involved—not only those which actually exist or are adoptable but those which have a purely ideational status and hence lie outside of P. The inclusion of E within C corresponds to the fact that efficient activities comprise part of a culture. The subset G of gainful resource processes is identical with the overlap, or logical product, of A and E.

Where, now, in this universe of resource processes are we to locate a resource complex? Where within the rectangle of Figure 1 are we to locate the set X'? (We shall defer to Chapter VI the problem of locating X''.) It is clear from our analysis of open field agriculture that we have there a resource complex which included both gainful and nongainful resource processes. Moreover, both of these sets of elements seem to have been necessary to the complex—"necessary" in the sense that they manifested some psychological incentives in the medieval resource user that have their counterpart in every social order. In this respect, our findings are considerably more restrictive than those of Chapter IV. There, of course, we went no further than to refute the two contrary hypotheses: $X' < -G$ and $X' < G$. Our present hypothesis affirms that X' must lie in both G and $-G$. This, to be sure, is a hypothesis whose universal truth we have in no sense established but whose meaningfulness has at least been supported by our illustrative case of open field agriculture.

In a provisional way, then, we may formalize our hypothesis as follows: First, we shall specify a set L of resource practices which have the property of appearing to the resource user as being more likely to be performed by his fellows than other practices. The property L is thus a phenomenal one, residing in the anticipations which the individual resource user has of the behavior of his fellows. More than this, it is a corollary to the objective conformity on the part of a population of resource users to the practices which comprise their resource complex. All conforming practices would have the property L; some nonconforming practices might have it but others would not.[31] The complement of L is comprised of all those processes which appear to the resource user as not more likely in the behavior of other resource users. This set $-L$, therefore, is inclusive of "as likely," "less likely," and "not likely," though for the sake of readability we shall generally render the symbol $-L$ as "nonlikely." Together L and $-L$ define a dichotomous attribute (a simplified scale or "variable")[32] which is differentiated by a cutting point that can only be located in terms of *ad hoc* empirical considerations.

The set L, of course, is a proper subset of the set A of adoptable resource processes. In other words, only adoptable processes are going to be likely ones, yet not *all* adoptable processes will be likely ones. Consistency with other activities in a culture is a necessary but not a necessary and sufficient condition for individuals' perception of a resource process as being likely. Moreover, if we may tentatively generalize from our single case of open field agriculture, the set L intersects with, but is not identical with, the set G of gainful resource processes, which is itself a subset of A. There are, that is, some resource practices lying outside G which fall within L: intermixed land holdings and manorial land and labor fixities, for example. Other resource practices, however, lie within both G and L: the use of horses along with oxen, and the use of both two-field and three-field rotations, for instance. Still other processes lie within G but lie outside L: such as the cultivation of root crops and the free alienation of land, neither of which were ever approved in open field agriculture. G and L thus represent two different partitions of A, a fact which may be more plainly expressed in the statement that what is gainful and what is likely are two different but not exclusive things.

In terms of L, it now becomes possible to specify in a fairly sure way the location of a resource complex X' with respect to the sets P, A, and G (the sets of possible, adoptable and gainful processes, respectively). X', we may hypothesize, is a proper subset of L, corresponding to the fact that every one of its practices has a high degree of phenomenal likelihood in the anticipations of each participant in the resource complex. More than this, it includes all those elements of G which G has in common with L, corresponding to the fact that some elements of a resource complex are both phenomenally likely and economically gainful. However, X' is by no means confined to the intersection of G and L; some of its elements lie outside of G, within $-G$, corresponding to the fact that some elements of a resource complex are phenomenally likely but are not economically gainful. Specifically:

$$A > G > (G \cdot L) < X' < L < A.$$

A resource complex X' is thus to be located somewhere between L and $G \cdot L$: all of its elements lie within L, some (but not all) of them lie within $G \cdot L$, and it includes all of

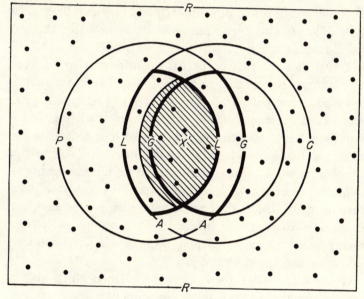

Figure 2.

the elements of $G \cdot L$ (see Figure 2). Those of its elements which are outside $G \cdot L$ are in $-G$. In short, a resource complex is comprised of the two subsets of practices:

$$(G \cdot L) \vee (-G \cdot L).$$

This formulation conforms to our empirical finding that a resource complex X' includes elements from both G and $-G$. In addition, it "explains" the existence of those elements of X' which lie outside G by expressing them as a function of the property L. The elements of X' may thus be viewed as a resultant of two contrary sets of forces: the incentive in every resource user to employ additional processes that are gainful to him (G); and the incentive in every resource user to employ all those processes which are generally observed in his community (L) and to which he expects to be held accountable. Somewhat metaphorically, then, G and L may be viewed as antipodes with reference to which X' constitutes itself. A perpetual *Spannung* exists between these antipodes, reflected in the individual resource user as an ambivalence with respect to the range of adoptable processes which confront him. His conformity is willing, but it is nonetheless "conformity," and as such it implies some latent inclination on his part to do otherwise. A resource complex, it would seem, predicates of its human agents an accurate perception of likelihood and an inaccurate judgment of gainfulness; they must have learned the lesson of Xenocrates' dictum: *"ut id sua sponte facerent, quod cogerentur facere legibus"* ("to do of their own accord what they are compelled to do by the law").[33]

We now reach the question of the balance which may or may not obtain between those elements of a resource complex which lie within G and those which lie within $-G$. We have seen that the existence of practices lying outside G is attributable to the incentive to observe processes which are observed by other members of a given social order. This incentive leads the individual to accept bounds to his preference for additional gainful resource processes. Are there limits, now, to this socially generated willingness to employ some inefficient practices and to abstain from some efficient ones? Speaking in graphic terms, how far into L, and outside of G, can X' extend, and how far too can X' be extended into G, outside of L? This is a question that can only be settled by an appeal to history, wherein we may observe changes in the composition of a resource complex.

NOTES

1. George Caspar Homans, *English Villagers of the Thirteenth Century* (Cambridge, Mass.: Harvard University Press, 1941), chap. iii; A. G. Tansley, *The British Islands and their Vegetation* (Cambridge: Cambridge University Press, 1939), pp. 178-79.

2. Howard Levi Gray, *English Field Systems* (Cambridge, Mass.: Harvard University Press, 1915), p. 40; Homans, *op. cit.*, p. 90.

3. G. V. Jacks and R. O. Whyte, *Vanishing Lands* (New York: Doubleday, Doran and Co., Inc., 1939), pp. 91-92; E. Estyn Evans, "The Ecology of Peasant Life in Western Europe," in William L. Thomas, Jr. (ed.), *Man's Role in Changing the Face of the Earth* (Chicago: University of Chicago Press, 1956), p. 228.

4. Homans, *op. cit.*, p. 41.

5. P. Vinogradoff, *The Growth of the Manor* (London: Swan Sonnenschein and Co. Ltd., 1905), p. 313.

6. C. S. and C. S. Orwin, *The Open Fields* (Oxford: the Clarendon Press, 1938), p. 157.

7. Homans, *op. cit.*, pp. 76-77; Gray, *op. cit.*, p. 9.

8. Orwin, *op. cit.*, pp. 32-34; cf. Homans, *op. cit.*, pp. 92-93.

9. Orwin, *op. cit.*, pp. 40-49; 56-57; Vinogradoff, *op. cit.*, pp. 200-1; Gray, *op. cit.*, pp. 8-9; Robert Trow-Smith, *English Husbandry* (London: Faber and Faber Ltd., 1951), p. 46; cf. Homans, *op. cit.*, p. 93, for reservations on this analysis.

10. Sir John Clapham, *A Concise Economic History of Britain from the Earliest Times to 1750* (Cambridge: Cambridge University Press, 1949), pp. 46-47.

11. M. E. Seebohm, *The Evolution of the English Farm* (Cambridge, Mass.: Harvard University Press, 1927), pp. 165-69.

12. *Ibid.*, p. 108.

13. Orwin, *op. cit.*, pp. 56-57.

14. E. Lipson, *An Introduction to the Economic History of England* (London: A. & C. Black Ltd., 1915), I, pp. 66-8; Vinogradoff, *op. cit.*, p. 182.

15. Orwin, *op. cit.*, pp. 156-67.

16. On the genesis and significance of alienative dispositions in the personality, see Talcott Parsons and Edward A. Shils, "Values, Motives, and Systems of Action," in Parsons *et al.*, *Toward a General Theory of Action* (Cambridge, Mass.: Harvard University Press, 1951), p. 157 and *passim.*

17. Charles Parain, "The Evolution of Agricultural Technique," in J. H. Clapham and Eileen Power (eds.), *The Cambridge Economic History of Europe from the Decline of the Roman Empire* (Cambridge: Cambridge University Press, 1941), I, 145.

18. This is indeed the distinguishing feature of legal norms as distinct from moral norms. In the latter there is only an acknowledged subject of *duty;* in the former, on the other hand, there is an acknowledged subject of duty and an acknowledged subject of *right,* viz., persons who can legitimately demand conformity on the part of others. For a systematic analysis of this and related distinctions, see Pitirim A. Sorokin, *Society, Culture, and Personality* (New York: Harper and Bros., 1947), pp. 71-85.

19. Georg Jellinek, *Allgemeine Staatslehre* (Berlin: O. Häring, 1900), pp. 307-10.

20. Lord Ernle, *English Farming Past and Present* (4th ed.; London: Longmans, Green and Co. Ltd., 1927), p. 13.

21. Parain, *op. cit.*, pp. 133-34.

22. Orwin, *op. cit.*, pp. 49-50.

23. Parain, *op. cit.*, pp. 129-31.

24. Lipson, *op. cit.*, p. 67.

25. Ernle, *op. cit.*, pp. 71, 108; L. Dudley Stamp, *The Land of Britain: its Use and Misuse* (London: Longmans, Green and Co. Ltd., 1948), p. 48.

26. Nellie Neilson, "Medieval Agrarian Society in its Prime: England," in J. H. Clapham and Eileen Power (eds.), *The Cambridge Economic History of Europe from the Decline of the Roman Empire* (Cambridge: Cambridge University Press, 1941), I, 442; E. A. Kosminsky, *Studies in the Agrarian History of England in the Thirteenth Century,* trans. Ruth Kisch (Oxford: Basil Blackwell and Mott Ltd., 1956), p. 84.

27. Vinogradoff, *op. cit.*, pp. 208-9; 309.

28. Homans, *op. cit.*, pp. 195, 203; Ernle, *op. cit.*, p. 38.

29. R. H. Tawney, *The Agrarian Problem in the Sixteenth Century* (London: Longmans, Green and Co. Ltd., 1912), p. 130.

30. "Possible," that is, relative to some stated unit of macro-time and to some stated parameters of extra-environmental influence.

31. Hence, likelihood is not to be merely equated with custom or tradition.

32. On the methodology of defining dichotomous attributes and related concepts, see: Paul F. Lazarsfeld and Allen H. Barton, "Qualitative Measurement in the Social Sciences: Classification, Typologies, and Indices," in Daniel Lerner and Harold D. Lasswell (eds.), *The Policy Sciences* (Stanford, Calif.: Stanford University Press, 1951), chap. ix; and Allen H. Barton, "The Concept of Property Space in Social Research," pp. 40-53 in Paul F. Lazarsfeld and Morris Rosenberg (eds.), *The Language of Social Research* (Glencoe, Ill.: The Free Press, 1955).

33. Imputed to Xenocrates by Cicero, *De Re Publica*, trans. Clinton Walker Keyes, The Loeb Classical Library (Cambridge: Harvard University Press, 1928), pp. 16-17.

CHAPTER VI

THE SOCIAL DYNAMICS
OF A RESOURCE COMPLEX

> There is . . . a tendency for the
> contradictions implicit in the con-
> tents of the social mind to find
> their way to the surface.
> EDWARD ALSWORTH ROSS *

GOVERNMENTS WHICH SEEK TO CHANGE their people's
resource practices can be sure of one fact: not all of
those practices are, or ever will be, the result of "chance, or
love, or logic"; [1] most of them are rather attributable to a
moral necessity which is expressed in the willing conformity
of their human agents. This fact imposes firm limits on the
scope of planned resource development and conservation.

Yet the attitude of willing conformity has, as we know,
a dual aspect. It manifests a deeply rooted ambivalence in
the human being as a resource user, whereby he finds himself impelled toward two distinct (though not exclusive)
kinds of practices: the gainful and the likely. Productive

efficiency impels him toward the former; prudence in his relationships with fellow resource users impels him toward the latter. The one leads him to experiment and to invent; the other leads him to acquiesce and to preserve.

This dual aspect to willing conformity endows every resource complex with an inherent potential for change, and it endows it, too, with an inherent resistance to change. In this *coincidentia oppositorum* lies the key to the social dynamics of every resource complex. New resource processes which are perceived as gainful by a population of resource users have first to undergo a selective process that is imposed by the social order. If the new processes comport with the vested interest which every resource user has in the behavior of his fellows, they will be readily incorporated into the existing resource complex. If, however, they threaten this vested interest, they will be resisted. Should the resistance be successful, the new process will fail of acceptance; if it is unsuccessful, the resource complex itself will be forthwith changed into another and different complex.

We have already seen, in the case of *citemene* agriculture, that a resource complex can have considerable tolerance for change and yet maintain its structural identity.[2] We have also seen, again in the *citemene* case, that there is always a break point beyond which further change will carry the complex into a structurally different order. We have now to inquire more closely into the nature of this break point. How, and under what formal conditions, does a resource complex change into another kind of entity? How much change can a resource complex undergo and yet retain its structural identity? These are questions that can be answered, though only in an illustrative way, by a further consideration of the case which we have described in our preceding chapter. Having seen there the ambivalent disposition which medieval English farmers had toward the practices which comprised their open field resource complex, let us now trace the developments by which this complex came to its end. Let us see how open field farming changed over a period of some five centuries, as exogenous factors afforded a release of previously inhibited incentives in its human agents. Let us see, too, how this complex finally reached a limit beyond which it became an altogether different entity.

Even as late as the fifteenth century, open field farming remained an unmistakably viable resource system. The gainful and the likely were mutually accommodated and there was, in Tawney's words, ". . . a happy balance between the forces of custom and the forces of economic enterprise, . . ." [3] The effect of the complex upon the land, to be sure, is not altogether clear. Fallowing was the only soil conserving practice which medieval farmers consistently employed; by means of it the land was afforded a rest every second or third year. Sheep and cattle provided some manure, though this cannot have been a significant factor because of the limited number of animals that any community was able to maintain through the feed-deficient winters. Also marl (a clayey soil containing carbonate of lime) was now and then applied to the highly acid land, thereby increasing the availability of plant nutrients. [4] Centuries of cultivation may here and there have depleted the soil of its fertility, but the evidence for this is by no means compelling. [5] On the whole, open field agriculture appears to have reasonably well maintained the capability of the land. [6]

Yet from the fourteenth century onward, English agricultural writers were uniform in their criticism of open field farming. What occasioned this criticism? What developments in English economic life led to so altered a perception of opportunities for gain and to so different an evaluation of customary rights and duties? The answer is to be found in the expansion of trade and manufacturing which attended the opening of trade routes in the Mediterranean, Baltic, and North seas after the eleventh century.[7] This expansion of trade and manufacturing offered a new source of tax revenue to English kings, who proceeded to actively promote, first, the exporting of raw wool and, later, the manufacturing of woolen cloth.[8] Thus, an essentially political decision, bearing upon open field communities throughout England, presented new opportunities for gain to peasants and to lords alike. Meanwhile, the same expansion of trade and manufacturing gave impetus to the growth of the towns and cities of England—particularly those situated in the more accessible districts of the South and East. The trading and manufacturing interests of these towns naturally gave them a stake in larger markets, greater mass purchasing power, and a mobile labor force. With reference to these aims, open field farming, with its diseconomic fixities of productive factors, was quite incompatible.[9] Furthermore, the growing towns and cities created a demand for grain and animal products which open field farming, geared as it was to the subsistence needs of its participants, was poorly equipped to meet.[10]

These new urban interests, combined with the interests of the English kings, represented elements wholly external to open field farming as a resource complex. Yet, given force by successive statutes and other politico-economic decisions, they attained an importance which eventually upset the medieval balance between gainful and nongainful resource practices. Meanwhile, the political stability of England, with its centralized monarchy and its well established royal courts, created a situation which was further conducive to production for the market. Landholders enjoyed a fair measure of confidence that long-range investments which they might make in rearranging productive factors for cash farming could be recouped with profit.[11]

A politico-economic environment was thus created which favored the expansion of production for the market. Yet open field agriculture had been organized around a subsistence economy, in which most of the product of the land was locally consumed. It was a resource complex that afforded only limited substitution between productive factors. As such, it thwarted the efforts of its human agents to capitalize upon the new opportunities of a market economy. As these new opportunities reached ever larger sectors of the English population, the motivation of resource users to conform to their open field practices was affected. The security which they had enjoyed in their personal relationships through faithful observance of those practices came to be regarded as hardly worth the economic inefficiency which they now entailed. A phenomenal imbalance resulted between those resource processes which were not gainful and those which were gainful. The nature of this imbalance, and its historical development, must now engage us in somewhat greater detail.

As early as the twelfth century, English farmers had begun to experiment with rearrangements of their intermixed land holdings. Individual peasants would now and then consolidate their scattered strips of land into discrete holdings on which customary resource practices would be somewhat varied. More frequently, manorial lords would consolidate their own holdings (the so-called "demesnes") into solid blocks of land which would then be privately operated. Fragments of communally-held waste land would occasionally be appropriated for private cultivation. Discrete holdings were sometimes partitioned out of the open fields for limited, agreed upon periods of time, following which they would again revert to open fields.[12] In some communities, there were experiments with four-field rotations in place of three- or two-field rotations, the result being more cropland but less fallow.[13] Occasionally a group of open field farmers would agree among themselves to a permanent division of their open fields into discrete, individual farmsteads which would then be privately operated.[14] Leases, loans and exchanges of parcels of land became an increasingly prevalent activity during the thirteenth century.[15] A tendency, too, developed for land to concentrate in the hands of an ever smaller proportion of peasants, with a concomitant economic differentiation between the members of open field communities.[16]

But it was the manorial lords, generally more aware than the peasantry of new opportunities for gain, who figured most prominently in the rearrangement and consolidation of intermixed land holdings. During the thirteenth century, prices for wool and food rose steadily, owing to the demand created by England's growing towns and cities as well as by the overseas cloth manufacturers of Flanders. In response to the opportunities thus presented, the manorial lords undertook to free their holdings from the rigidity of open field practices.[17] They consolidated the scattered strips of land which, on every manor, had customarily been worked for them by the peasants who were bound to such labor duty. On their newly consolidated holdings, the lords developed a distinct *demesne economy*,[18] the production of which was geared to the market rather than to local subsistence needs. Labor was provided either by unfree peasants, who more than ever were impressed into the compulsory service of the lords, or by free laborers who were hired on a contractual basis. Frequently, the unfree peasants were permitted and even encouraged to substitute cash payments for compulsory labor, thus affording the lords greater flexibility in organizing their productive activities.[19] Frequently, too, lords would lease out their demesnes to renters on a strictly contractual basis.[20]

A shrewd, calculating population of resource users was thus arising, whose advantage lay in evading or disregarding customary resource practices and in devising new ones that would yield greater revenues. To meet their interest in more gainful resource practices, a whole literature on agriculture and estate management made its appearance.[21] Yet open field agriculture was by no means finished: from the beginning, it offered stubborn resistance to all deviations from its practices. The innovations of the thirteenth century did not, therefore, represent a break from its essential character. Fields were still rotated between cultivation and fallow; peasants still farmed their scattered strips of land along with their plow team mates; and oxen, as well as sheep and horses, were still communally grazed in the open fields. Thirteenth century resource practices could still be represented as falling wholly within the set X' of open field practices. The new innovations, for the most part, represented adaptations of this resource complex to the requirements of an expanding market economy. Hence, the imbalance between gainful and nongainful practices had not yet exceeded the tolerance of the complex for change.

During the fourteenth and fifteenth centuries, however, the trend toward consolidation of holdings and farming "in severalty" (i.e., farming apart from the co-operative open field routine) continued and accelerated. A decline in grain and wool prices after 1320 gave impetus to the leasing of manorial demesnes to free tenants, generally in large blocks and for increasingly long periods of time. These holdings were then operated as farmsteads whose activities could be freely adapted to varying market opportunities. Their tenants became the precursors of the prosperous scientific farmers of the sixteenth century.[22] Meanwhile, the compulsory labor of unfree peasants, too, was more and more being replaced by that of free wage earners, affording thus still further opportunity for advantageous variation of productive factors.[23] Peasants also continued to make deals with each other, often at variance with open field custom; at various times and places they consolidated their scattered strips of land, bought or leased holdings from their neighbors, sublet portions of land to other neighbors,[24] and even suspended their mutual rights to graze animals in the open fields following harvest.[25] Free tenants and the smaller landlords, being somewhat on the margin of the manorial system, seem to have been especially prominent in these developments. In all such ways, land and labor were being rendered ever more mobile factors of production which might be variously combined in proportions that would increase productive efficiency. Fields could be more efficiently laid out; crops could be better adapted to soil types; incompetent neighbors could be left to themselves; and a fluid relationship could be achieved between farm operations and market opportunities.[26]

The imbalance which had long been developing within open field agriculture had now reached a critical magnitude. Practices were being added to the complex which, by virtue of their efficiency, obviously lay within the set of gainful practices. Yet they so violated the expectations which open field farmers had of one another's behavior as to occasion endless disputation, breaches of faith, litigation, and abuse of weaker by stronger members of the community.[27] As resource practices became more individualized, it became increasingly difficult for a wronged or offended person to find allies who would assist him in imposing sanctions on the nonconformist—whether this be a neighbor or the manorial lord himself. One hardly knew what to expect of his fellows: when they would conform, when they would evade, when they would flout customary practices.

A thoroughgoing ambiguity had thus entered into personal relationships by which it became less and less possible for individuals to depend upon others' observance of particular resource processes. Not only did others' behavior become less predictable in fact, but it failed to correspond with what a person felt he had a right to expect of others. With security in personal relationships thus destroyed, the whole incentive to inhibit one's propensity for gainful resource processes was removed.[28] A latent inclination in all resource users to experiment with gainful processes, even when beyond the margin of others' tolerance, became increasingly manifest in actual behavior. Nongainful processes, which had previously been followed for reasons of prudence, could now be abandoned with impunity. Resource users lost their ambivalent attitude toward the practices which comprised their open field complex. They proceeded to exchange security for efficiency. The corollary of all this was a disintegration of open field agriculture as a resource complex. In its place, a congeries of resource processes, distinguished by a calculating opportunism rather than by a willing conformity on the part of its human agents, came to dominate much of the English Midlands. This new entity we shall designate by the symbol X''. Its formal properties can be most clearly seen in the next development of English land use, viz., commercial sheep farming.

For several centuries, the open field complex had included among its practices the pasturing of sheep on fallow and harvested land. Every peasant, along with every lord of a manor, was allowed to graze a fixed quota of sheep, the number of which was proportional to his holdings of land. By the late thirteenth century, however, the market for wool had become so well developed that these quotas had come to be regarded as unduly restrictive of personal opportunities for gain. Peasants and lords alike took to running herds of sheep in excess of their quotas and well beyond the land's carrying capacity. By the fourteenth century, open fields were here and there being divided up, then enclosed and converted to pasture.[29] This latter trend accelerated during the fifteenth century, stimulated by the growth of domestic cloth manufacturing in England.[30] With a stable and expanding wool market thus assured them, the manorial lords in particular embarked on a massive conversion of their estates from grain to sheep.[31] Townspeople, too, looking for safe and lucrative investments, began to buy up manorial estates and to convert them into commercial sheep farms.[32]

The impact of sheep farming upon open field agriculture was disastrous. The two sets of resource processes had altogether different requirements of land and labor. Moreover, they remained entirely dissociated from each other. A system of mixed farming, in which tillage and grazing might be integrated into a single resource complex, had yet to be discovered by English resource users.[33] Sheep farming, as practiced between the fourteenth and eighteenth centuries, required compact plots of land, neatly fenced in and put to grass, in place of the old open fields which had been rotated between crops and fallow. Moreover, it required only a small population of hired shepherds in place of a sizeable population of land bound peasants. As the conversion from grain to grass gained momentum a wave of evictions swept over the rural countryside of England, reaching its peak between 1440 and 1520, leaving abandoned communities and a destitute proletariat in its wake.[34]

The manner by which sheep farming thus succeeded open field farming reveals its fundamental lack of viability. The peasantry, for the most part, did not willingly abandon their holdings of land. Their interest lay, rather, in maintaining the "collective bargain" which had traditionally linked them with their manorial lords. But this bargain was no longer advantageous to the lords. Relative to the new opportunities afforded the lords by the expanding market for wool, the peasantry now constituted a superfluous labor force. From the standpoint of the manorial lords, there was little point to being ambivalent any longer about open field practices; the advantages of observing those practices had become so negligible compared with the advantages of violating them that the complex had lost the essential condition of its viability, viz., the willing conformity of its human agents, or at least of the manorial lords. Only the peasants retained some ambivalent disposition toward their open field practices which, as we have argued, is the *sine qua non* of every viable set of resource practices. To them, the advantages of conformity (and of holding the lords to conformity) still outweighed the advantages of nonconformity.[35]

Thus, a clear conflict of interest existed between the peasants and the manorial lords. In this conflict, the government sought initially to check the conversion of land from tillage to pasture. But the balance of political forces, particularly as between central and local authorities, was such as to nullify the effect of restrictive legislation.[36] Manorial lords proceeded with their conversions, using such means as exorbitant fees, persuasion, fraud, and outright coercion to rid their estates of a now redundant labor force.[37] A new set of resource processes came to dominate the English Midlands, not wholly displacing open field agriculture but effectively destroying the conditions of its viability. By the seventeenth century the customary expectations which open field farmers had previously had of one another's behavior had lost much of their force.

Yet open field processes persisted as cultural survivals

right down to the nineteenth century; indeed, they are not entirely unknown in England today. But they could no longer be said to constitute a resource complex. Their essential character is aptly suggested by the term *congeries*.[38] By this term, we shall designate any set of resource processes X'' which includes among its elements some processes that lie outside the set L of likely processes though lying inside the set G of gainful processes. The range of X'' corresponds to the logical sum of the subsets

$$(G \cdot L) \vee (-G \cdot L) \vee (G \cdot -L),$$

these terms denoting corresponding subsets of the gainful and likely processes, the nongainful and likely processes, and the gainful and nonlikely processes. The proposition $X'' > X'$ expresses the fact that a resource congeries may subsume a resource complex.

Inclusion in a resource system of all three of these subsets $(G \cdot L)$, $(-G \cdot L)$ and $(G \cdot -L)$ constitutes something of an anomaly. It means that some gainful processes are being employed (those comprising $G \cdot -L$) even though they are perceived as nonlikely in the behavior of others, indicating that the sanctions which inhere in the reactions that every resource user predicates of his fellows to his own actions are no longer effective. It means, too, that some nongainful processes (those comprising $-G \cdot L$) are being employed for no other reason that that they give warrant to a resource user's claim, however ineffectual it may be as a sanction, that his fellows owe it to him to behave likewise. Such a combination of $G \cdot -L$ and $-G \cdot L$ means that a dissociation has occurred between the egoistic and the altruistic criteria by which resource users judge the value of various resource processes—a matter to which we are going to return at another place (Chapter IX).

A resource congeries X'', then, represents a breach with one of the minimum conditions of social order, viz., the ability of every member of a group to assign a high degree of likelihood to all the possible activities of that group.[39] In the absence of this minimum condition, there can be little basis in personal relationships for the maintenance of an ambivalent attitude toward a set of adoptable resource processes. Hence, in place of a willing commitment of resource users to just the two subsets $G \cdot L$ and $-G \cdot L$, there is a calculated involvement of resource users in the three subsets $G \cdot L$, $-G \cdot L$ and $G \cdot -L$. In place of an attitude of willing conformity, there is an attitude of calculating opportunism. A break point has been reached in which the tolerance of a resource complex for change has been exceeded and the structure itself has broken down. The new resource processes, structurally extraneous to the old complex X', constitute accretions to a population's repertoire of resource processes, and they yield an altogether different kind of entity X'' which lacks the invariance properties of its predecessor. This new entity, having no determinate structure, can offer little resisance to further change. In an increasing degree, resource users are able to experiment and innovate with impunity. Thus an amorphous, dynamic, and changeable set of resource processes succeeds to a determinate, static, and rigid set of resource processes. The "happy balance" between custom and enterprise is gone.

By the eighteenth century, then, English open field agriculture had become something of an anachronism—a survival which was poorly articulated with the newer resource processes that were entering the system. To be sure, open fields comprised, even at the close of the seventeenth century, about one half of the arable land of England.[40] But alongside their subsistence-oriented, co-operatively managed units of production, there were now the market-oriented, individually managed farmsteads which had succeeded the old manorial demesnes and the free tenant holdings. Between these two sectors of economic enterprise there could be little articulation. The latter, run for the most part by prosperous tenants who found themselves driven by competitive rents to maximizing the efficiency of their processes, became instruments of agricultural experimentation and innovation.[41] To meet their needs, a new agricultural literature developed, addressed to them and their landlords, and advocating such novel resource processes as the use of root crops, the adoption of farm implements, and the use of new crop rotations.[42]

Throughout the sixteenth century, the English Midlands continued to undergo conversion from grain to sheep.[43] But after the middle of this century, and through the seventeenth century, there were some reconversions of land back to grain.[44] By the eighteenth century, such reconversions had become paramount except in the comparatively remote Inner Midlands.[45] The occasion for these shifting trends in land use lay in the play of market forces and in the impact of political decisions. Thus between 1490 and 1572, apart from a few exceptional years, wool prices were relatively more advantageous to farmers than grain prices. After 1572, however, grain prices improved steadily and they eventually shifted the "balance of advantage" from sheep farming back to grain farming.[46] This trend was reinforced a century later by legislation which imposed a tariff on foreign grain and put a bounty on the export of domestic grain, thereby shifting the balance of advantage even further toward grain relative to sheep. At least part of the motivation behind this legislation seems to have been the desire of royalty to curry political favor with the land-lord class.[47] Such vulnerability of resource users to politico-economic decisions is a phenomenon which we are going to consider more fully in Chapter VIII. For the present, it is enough to have taken note of the phenomenon and to have observed its connection with a resource congeries in which the use to which resources are put becomes a function of gainfulness alone, rather than of gainfulness and likelihood together.

With resource users now so largely preoccupied with productive efficiency rather than with prudence in their traditional social relationships, there ensued a whole series of radical agricultural innovations, beginning in the late seventeenth century and extending well into the nineteenth century. As early as the sixteenth century there had been experimentation with various rotations of grains and grasses done with a view to reducing the unproductive fallow period on enclosed fields.[48] Then, in the early eighteenth century, there came the realization that root crops, which had long been cultivated as garden vegetables, would make excellent winter forage for animals. At about the same time, grass seeding was introduced which once and for all freed resource users from dependence on their scarce supply of meadow land for hay.[49] Neither of these developments had been feasible so long as open field peasants were able to enforce their traditional prerogatives concerning the common grazing of harvested fields and meadow land. Even as late as 1837, most of the English Midlands were still being farmed just as they had been for centuries before. Lord Ernle has aptly characterized this resource congeries in his epigrammatic observation that: "A hundred farmers plodded along the Elizabethan road, while a solitary neighbour marched in the track of the twentieth century." [50] But with the gradual breakdown of the social sanctions for traditional grazing prerogatives, particularly on lands which had been removed from the open field routine, the newer processes became incorporated into an evolving congeries of English resource processes.[51]

The significance of the root crops (particularly the turnip) and artificial grasses lay in the fact that they allowed farmers to carry many more animals through the winter, thereby increasing the supply of animal products and providing more manure with which to improve the fertility of the soil. The effects of this were far reaching. No longer did from one-third to one-half of the land have to lie idle in unproductive fallow every year. So long as grain crops were properly rotated with grasses and root crops, the soil could be put to productive use year in and year out with no impairment of its fertility. Larger crops could be raised, more animals supported, and improved varieties of both grains and animals developed.[52]

Of course the adoption of root crops and artificial grasses led eventually to the development of corresponding new technicways—new work routines, new disciplines, new social incentives. The root crops, for instance, required hoeing in place of plowing: soil had to be clean tilled and well worked if it were to yield a satisfactory harvest.[53] For this purpose, the use of the plow team was poorly suited. A whole new organization of personal relationships had therefore to evolve before the new system could be properly called a resource complex. Not until the middle of the nineteenth century did mixed farming approach this status, and then it was abruptly terminated by the appearance in the British market of cheap American wheat and beef.

During the century and a half preceding this debacle, little remained of the ambivalent commitment of resource users to both gainful and nongainful processes. During this period, too, little remained of security in personal relationships. Large landholders gained in political influence, open field farmers were gradually eliminated, and small, independent farmers declined in numbers (especially after 1815).[54] A resource congeries prevailed whose ever changing complement of processes responded only to the exigencies of the market. When wool and grain prices dropped, land was shifted to cattle. When grain prices rose, waste lands were put to the plow.[55]

The Napoleonic period, for instance, was one of rising food prices. From 1760 to 1813 there was a heavy flow of capital into agriculture, with new crops, improved livestock, and better farm implements coming into use.[56] Land became a profitable investment. Then, in 1813, prices collapsed. A profound agricultural depression ensued which led to the abandonment of farms, the reversion of cropland to waste, and the disappearance of most of the smaller landholders.[57] Land gravitated to large capitalist farmers and to businessmen.[58] By 1830, better prices for farm products resulting from the growing urban and industrial market made agriculture once again profitable. Cultivation of grain was extended into marginal lands; farm implements were further improved; better breeds of stock were perfected; and chemical fertilizers were discovered.[59] Then, in the 1870's, cheap American wheat and beef reached the British Isles and brought a precipitous decline in British mixed farming, predicated as it had been on high domestic food prices.[60]

In all these vicissitudes, there is evident that "husbandry of opportunism" which invariably characterizes a resource congeries.[61] In the face of a volatile environment of politico-economic decisions, resource users acted with "willingness" but not with "conformity." Efficiency rather than prudence was their norm. Profit rather than sustenance was their goal. Innovation rather than preservation was their means. Their resource processes could be placed, with little or no ambivalence, high on a scale of productive efficiency; they could not be so unambiguously placed on a scale of likelihood. Hence, the two basic requisites of a viable set of resource practices were missing, viz.: (1) an ambivalent commitment of resource users to both gainful and non-gainful practices, and (2) an unambiguous perception by resource users of likelihood in one another's resource practices.

A resource complex, it would seem, is predicated on some degree of stability in its structural parameters. When these quantities change beyond a critical magnitude, as they may when new trade routes are opened, or when technical discoveries are made, or when the components of a social order in any other way alter, that fragile balance between gainful and likely practices which characterizes a resource complex is upset. The incentive to employ gainful processes, which has previously been held in bounds by each person's prudential regard for the expectations of his fellows (and hence for the long run security of his own rights), can now press beyond the limits of social tolerance; the penalties which are thus incurred, in the way of jeopardy to one's customary rights, are no longer of sufficient consequence to deter the individual from employing the more gainful processes. As new processes are thereupon added to a population's complement of resource processes, a break point is eventually reached beyond which the new processes so far exceed social expectations that all dependability in people's behavior breaks down. At this point, the resource complex becomes a resource congeries. This entity, lacking the determinate structure of a resource complex, can offer little resistance to further change. New processes thereby come into use which reconstitute the very land itself and endow it, as it were, with new natural resources.

NOTES

* Edward Alsworth Ross, *Social Psychology* (New York: Macmillan Co., 1920), p. 355.

1. With apologies to Charles S. Peirce and to Morris R. Cohen. See Peirce's *Chance, Love, and Logic,* ed. Morris R. Cohen (New York: Harcourt, Brace and Co., 1923).

2. More precisely, for any resource complex there is an empirically admissible group of transformations which relate that complex to a set of complexes isomorphic with it. Hence, when referring to a tolerable change in *a* resource complex, we might better speak of an isomorphism between *two* complexes, that which existed before and that which existed after. For the sake of readability, however, this refinement will not be

observed in the present work. See Nicholas Rescher and Paul Oppenheim, "Logical Analysis of Gestalt Concepts," *British Journal for the Philosophy of Science,* VI (1955), 89-106.

3. R. H. Tawney, *The Agrarian Problem in the Sixteenth Century* (London: Longmans, Green and Co. Ltd., 1912), p. 136.

4. George Caspar Homans, *English Villagers of the Thirteenth Century* (Cambridge, Mass.: Harvard University Press, 1941), pp. 40-42; M. E. Seebohm, *The Evolution of the English Farm* (Cambridge, Mass.: Harvard University Press, 1927), pp. 186, 357; Charles Parain, "The Evolution of Agricultural Technique," in J. H. Clapham and Eileen Power (eds.), *The Cambridge Economic History of Europe from the Decline of the Roman Empire* (Cambridge: Cambridge University Press, 1941), I, 135.

5. E. C. K. Gonner, *Common Land and Inclosure* (London: Macmillan and Co. Ltd., 1912), p. 121. For an extreme view on the matter which appears not to have been sustained by more recent research, see: Harriett Bradley, *The Enclosures in England* ("Columbia University Studies in History, Economics and Public Law" [New York: Columbia University Press, 1918]), Vol. LXXX, No. 2.

6. Siegfried von Ciriacy-Wantrup, "Soil Conservation in European Farm Management," *Journal of Farm Economics,* XX (1938), 86-101; Sir John Clapham, *A Concise Economic History of Britain from the Earliest Times to 1750* (Cambridge: Cambridge University Press, 1949), p. 84.

7. Henri Pirenne, *Economic and Social History of Medieval Europe* (London: Kegan Paul, Trench, Trubner and Co. Ltd., 1936); Paul M. Sweezy, "The Transition from Feudalism to Capitalism," *Science and Society,* XIV (1950), 134-57; *idem,* "Communication," in *Science and Society,* XVII (1953), 158-64.

8. Max Weber, *General Economic History* (Glencoe, Ill.: The Free Press, 1950), p. 85.

9. *Ibid.,* pp. 93-95.

10. Sweezy, "The Transition . . . ."

11. Weber, *op. cit.,* pp. 73, 78.

12. Gonner, *op. cit.,* p. 38.

13. Howard Levi Gray, *English Field Systems* (Cambridge, Mass.: Harvard University Press, 1915), pp. 109-10.

14. Lord Ernle, *English Farming Past and Present* (4th ed.; London: Longmans, Green and Co. Ltd., 1927), p. 38.

15. Homans, *op. cit.,* pp. 18, 203; Tawney, *op. cit.,* p. 9.

16. E. A. Kosminsky, *Studies in the Agrarian History of England in the Thirteenth Century* (Oxford: Basil Blackwell and Mott Ltd., 1956), p. 254.

17. P. Vinogradoff, *The Growth of the Manor* (London: Swan Sonnenschein and Co. Ltd., 1905), p. 331.

18. Kosminsky, *op. cit.*, p. 325.

19. *Ibid.*, pp. 327-30; Ernle, *op. cit.*, p. 39.

20. W. Hasbach, *A History of the English Agricultural Labourer* (London: P. S. King and Son, 1908), p. 17; E. Lipson, *An Introduction to the Economic History of England* (London: A. & C. Black Ltd., 1915), I, 77-78; Nellie Neilson, "Medieval Agrarian Society in its Prime: England," in J. H. Clapham and Eileen Power (eds.), *The Cambridge Economic History of Europe from the Decline of the Roman Empire* (Cambridge: Cambridge University Press, 1941), I, 466.

21. Neilson, *op. cit.*, pp. 465-66.

22. Vinogradoff, *op. cit.*, p. 331; Seebohm, *op. cit.*, p. 187; H. O. Meredith, *Economic History of England* (5th ed.; London: Sir Isaac Pitman & Sons Ltd., 1949), p. 106.

23. Marion Gibbs, *Feudal Order* (London: Cobbett Press, 1949), pp. 134-36; Lipson, *op. cit.*, pp. 78-82.

24. Lipson, *op. cit.*, pp. 115-18.

25. *Ibid.*, pp. 115-18; Ernle, *op. cit.*, p. 39.

26. Gonner, *op. cit.*, pp. 308-18.

27. *Ibid.*, p. 360; Lipson, *op. cit.*, p. 118.

28. For systematic analyses of the conditions of conforming and non-conforming conduct see: Robert K. Merton, *Social Theory and Social Structure* (Glencoe, Ill.: The Free Press, 1949), chap. iv; Talcott Parsons and Edward A. Shils, in *Toward a General Theory of Action* (Cambridge, Mass.: Harvard University Press, 1951), Part II; Talcott Parsons, *The Social System* (Glencoe, Ill.: The Free Press, 1951), chaps. vi-vii.

29. Tawney, *op. cit.*, pp. 170-72; Neilson, *op. cit.*, p. 462.

30. Meredith, *op. cit.*, pp. 146-47.

31. Maurice Beresford, *The Lost Villages of England* (London: Lutterworth Press, 1954), p. 197.

32. Lipson, *op. cit.*, p. 129.

33. Ernle, *op. cit.*, pp. 57, 121-22.

34. Beresford, *op. cit.*, chap. iii.

35. Tawney, *op. cit.*, p. 130.

36. Beresford, *op. cit.*, pp. 130-32; Lipson, *op. cit.*, pp. 155-56.

37. Ernle, *op. cit.*, pp. 161-62; Tawney, *op. cit.*, p. 310.

38. A concept advanced by Pitirim A. Sorokin in his *Social and Cultural Dynamics* (New York: American Book Co., 1937 and 1941), Vol. IV, chap. i, and in his *Society, Culture, and Personality* (New York: Harper and Bros., 1947), chap. xvii.

39. Clyde Kluckhohn *et al.*, "Values and Value-Orientations in the Theory of Action," in Talcott Parsons and Edward A. Shils, *Toward a General Theory of Action* (Cambridge, Mass.: Harvard University Press, 1951), p. 400.

40. Ernle, *op. cit.,* pp. 132-33, 154.

41. Tawney, *op. cit.,* pp. 201-11, 216.

42. Naomi Riches, *The Agricultural Revolution in Norfolk* (Chapel Hill, N. C.: University of North Carolina Press, 1937), pp. 11-12; Seebohm, *op. cit.,* p. 241.

43. J. D. Gould, "Mr. Beresford and the Lost Villages: a Comment," *Agricultural History Review,* III, Part II (1955), 108-11.

44. Beresford, *op. cit.,* pp. 139, 184, 213-14; Gonner, *op. cit.,* p. 354; Ernle, *op. cit.,* p. 103.

45. Beresford, *op. cit.,* p. 245.

46. The expression is due to Beresford. See also Beresford, *op. cit.,* p. 426, fn. 10.

47. Hasbach, *op. cit.,* pp. 47-50.

48. Norman Scott Brien Gras, *A History of Agriculture in Europe and America* (New York: F. S. Crofts Co., 1925), pp. 36-38; Robert Trow-Smith, *English Husbandry* (London: Faber and Faber Ltd., 1951), p. 100; Gray, *op. cit.,* p. 404. On the social and cultural context of science and technology generally, in seventeenth century England, see: Robert K. Merton, *Science, Technology and Society in Seventeenth Century England,* Osiris (Bruges, Belgium, 1938), Vol. IV, Part II.

49. Bradley, *op. cit.,* p. 102; Gras, *op. cit.,* pp. 183-84; Riches, *op. cit.,* pp. 15-16.

50. Ernle, *op. cit.,* p. 358.

51. *Ibid.,* pp. 174-75; Gonner, *op. cit.,* pp. 318-19.

52. Seebohm, *op. cit.,* p. 279; Riches, *op. cit.,* pp. 15-16.

53. Gras, *op. cit.,* p. 209.

54. *Ibid.,* pp. 170-73. The routes by which open field agriculture disappeared were not the same in different countries, owing to the varying kinds of politico-economic decisions which were made as one country after another was opened up to world markets. See Weber, *op. cit.,* chaps. v-vi.

55. W. H. B. Court, *A Concise Economic History of Britain from 1750 to Recent Times* (Cambridge: Cambridge University Press, 1954), pp. 23, 35; Hasbach, *op. cit.,* pp. 55-56.

56. Ernle, *op. cit.,* pp. 207-15.

57. *Ibid.,* pp. 319-27.

58. Hasbach, *op. cit.,* pp. 103-6.

59. Ernle, *op. cit.,* pp. 346-66; Court, *op. cit.,* pp. 162-63, 204.

60. Court, *op. cit.,* pp. 204-5.

61. A phrase applied by Trow-Smith (*op. cit.,* p. 186) to the last fifty years of British agriculture but which, in a more general sense, can be applied to the last two centuries of British agriculture.

CHAPTER VII

THE DEVELOPMENT
OF NATURAL RESOURCES

> Human occupance of area, like
> other biotic phenomena, carries
> within itself the seed of its own
> transformation.
> DERWENT WHITTLESEY[1]

ANY PROGRAM of resource planning will have one of two objectives: that of developing natural resources, or that of conserving natural resources. While these objectives need not be mutually exclusive, they generally are. Moreover, the necessary conditions for achieving the one and the other are fundamentally unlike. The nature of this difference must now engage us.

As a preliminary to this undertaking we shall want to attach some fairly definite meanings to the words *development* and *conservation* insofar as these terms are applied to natural resources. We shall forego a review of the literature on this point and will simply propose two definitions which appear to subsume most other definitions of the terms and which have the requisite generality for a cross cultural approach to natural resources. Implicit in the two definitions is a conception of natural resources as landed capital, differing from other types of capital only in the relatively greater part which non-human events have played in their origin.[2] A natural resource p', then, may be viewed as a resource process p of P with which certain cultural activities c of C have been combined, this combination having the potential effect of decreasing the magnitude of scarcity which attaches to a people's activities. A natural resource is the organic or physical component of an adoptable resource process. Hence, the locus of a natural resource is in the set A of adoptable resource processes (p' ε A).[3]

A distinction may now be drawn between those resource processes which are adoptable by a population but are not used, and those resource processes which are actually employed by a population. By definition all natural resources belong to the set A of adoptable resource processes; employed natural resources belong to the more restricted subset $X < A$ of processes comprising a resource system.

Resource development, now, has to do with the conversion of inert natural processes into potential capital.[4] It is a conversion in which some elements p of P become so combined with some elements c of C as to contribute, at least potentially, toward decreasing the magnitude of scarcity attaching to a people's activities. In this conversion, p ε $-A$ becomes p' ε α, α being defined as that set of processes whose elements are outside A at some specified point in time and are inside A at some specified later point in time.

Any instance, of course, in which $p \, \varepsilon -A$ becomes $p' \, \varepsilon \, X$ is a special case of resource development, viz., that in which an inert natural process is put to actual use. The term "resource development" should not, however, be restricted to this special case. Generality beyond the conditions of Western capitalism would seem to require our including within the scope of the term any conversion of natural processes into natural resources, whether those resources are actually used or not. It is enough that the values and techniques of a people render certain elements of their habitat accessible to them at whatever time they may choose to exploit those elements.

In the case of *resource conservation*, on the other hand, the question can only be one of resources which are actually being employed by a population; to speak of conserving an unused (though adoptable) resource would be a redundancy. Moreover, where resource development is concerned with the creation of social capital, conservation is concerned with the maintenance of social capital. An employed natural resource which is subject to depletion will, in the course of its exhaustion, revert to an inert natural process which in that form is no longer available for a population's use. In this reversion, $p' \, \varepsilon \, X$ becomes $p \, \varepsilon -A$; as such, it is no longer a natural resource. Conservation consists of so reducing a people's standards of consumption that p' continues, for a longer time than otherwise, to be at least available and adoptable for that population—i.e., to remain within the set A and perhaps, though not necessarily, within the set X.[5]

In this and the succeeding chapter, we propose to examine some of the necessary conditions for resource development and resource use, deferring to Chapter IX a similar consideration of resource conservation. In all three chapters, we shall describe and analyze a single geographical example of resource use, with the intent of illustrating rather than proving some hypotheses concerning resource development and conservation. The case which we have selected is situated in the southernmost extremity of the High Plains of North America, in an area known as the southern High Plains, or the South Plains, of Texas and New Mexico. It is a case which affords, within the brief span of fifty years, a full panorama of the development, exploitation, and conservation of a strategic natural resource, groundwater. It is, moreover, an example about which there is an abundance of reliable documentary materials, both historical and contemporaneous. Finally, it is a case which throws into relief many of the problems which confront the resource planner and policy maker who seeks to improve upon the resource practices of a population.

Let us begin our account of the development of South Plains resources (groundwater in particular) by first noting some salient features of the area's resource processes in general. Following this, we shall state a formal hypothesis concerning one of the necessary conditions for the development of a natural resource. Then, in terms of this hypothesis, we shall consider in greater detail the development of South Plains groundwater as a natural resource.

The South Plains of Texas and New Mexico is a highly mechanized and irrigated agricultural area which has experienced phenomenally rapid economic growth. Situated in the treeless, semiarid grasslands of the American Southwest, its agricultural productivity today depends very largely on the exploitation of subterranean water by the use of deep irrigation wells. On the basis of this limiting resource, the South Plains has developed a resource congeries which can be most aptly characterized as a "husbandry of opportunism." [6] The unit of resource use in South Plains agriculture is, as in most of America, the farm—a family managed tract of land, owned in fee simple or leased on a crop-share basis, and, at least in principle, planted, cultivated, and harvested in whatever crops and by whatever system its individual operator may prefer. Resource processes in the South Plains have been quick to respond to varying politico-economic decisions: to changed market relationships, revised governmental policies, new technical developments, etc. Crops have been chosen almost wholly in terms of what they will bring on the market, with cotton, wheat, and grain sorghums having proved the most consistently profitable ones. Of the South Plains farmer it may truly be said that he ". . . is the cultivator plus the business man in one. . . . He has one eye on the farm and the other on the market." [7]

The congeries of processes which today characterizes the South Plains is the most recent variant of a succession of resource congeries which have dominated the area.[8] Early Mexican sheep ranching was displaced by Anglo cattle ranching in the late 1870's.[9] A limited supplemental agriculture accompanied these pastoral uses of land. Cotton was first introduced in 1888 and grain sorghum in 1886.[10] Then, with the extension of the railroad into the South Plains in 1907, a veritable revolution in resource processes took place. With supplies and a market now assured them, a wave of newly arriving settlers bought up tracts of land

and introduced a cotton-grain sorghum-wheat agricultural economy.[11] A good deal of experimentation with crops and equipment was undertaken by these early settlers: millet was tried, became popular by 1904, and then declined in favor after 1910; corn was brought into the area by migrants from the corn belt, but it too declined after 1910.[12] Various kinds of planting, mowing, and harvesting machines were devised in an effort to rationalize farm operations in a labor-scarce region.[13] Irrigation from deep wells was first attempted in 1911 but proved at that time too expensive an operation.[14]

With the close of the first World War, cotton prices rose to the point that cattle ranching ceased to be a competitive land use. Ranches throughout the South Plains were broken up and sold to farmers who once again were arriving in droves.[15] By the 1920's cotton, wheat, and grain sorghum had become fairly well established as the basic crops of the South Plains.[16] During this period there was continued experimentation with labor-saving machinery. The combine, or harvester-thresher, had been introduced in the South Plains in 1919.[17] By 1926, three additional technological developments were introduced: the all-purpose tractor, admirably adapted to the cultivation of row crops; the two-row lister-planter and cultivator; and the mechanical cotton harvester, more generally known as the stripper.[18] Thereafter, tractor power quickly took the place of horse power, and multi-row equipment rapidly displaced the older one-row equipment. Irrigation, too, long dormant since its abortive 1911 development, again came into favor, stimulated particularly by the severe drought of 1934-35. In the course of the last twenty years, it has almost wholly transformed South Plains farming from a precarious dryland operation to a highly productive irrigation enterprise. In the analysis which presently follows, it will be the process of irrigation which is to serve as our primary focus of interest. We shall want to bear in mind the fact, however, that irrigation is only one more new resource process in a whole series of new processes that have characterized the South Plains ever since its shift from a pastoral to an agricultural type of resource congeries.[19]

The annual cycle of South Plains resource processes begins in the fall, shortly after the previous year's crops have been harvested. At this time, tractor-powered stalk cutters are driven through the fields, chopping up the old cotton and sorghum stalks, after which the residue is plowed into the ground. Shortly thereafter, the land is bedded in long, straight rows, or if necessary it may first be "flat broken" so that altogether new beds can be formed. Beds and furrows are made with a tractor-mounted plow known as the lister, which makes as many as four furrows in a single run down the field. Cultivation by means of tractor-mounted disks may be necessary before the spring planting. By January or February, the irrigation pumps are turned on, and the beds are given an initial pre-planting watering, frequently followed by an additional irrigation before planting in order to thoroughly wet the top soil. In late April or May, as soon as the ground has become sufficiently warm, the cotton is planted by tractor-mounted planters which can seed four rows at a time, frequently applying fertilizer in the same operation.

In a week or so, the seedlings begin to emerge from the soil. Shortly thereafter, hand hoeing and mechanical cultivation become necessary in order to clear out weed growth. Irrigation wells are turned on at intervals ranging from two to eight weeks, most farmers watering their crops three or four times between planting and harvesting. Insectides are applied mechanically with tractor-mounted dusters as often as a dozen times during the summer. In September, chemical defoliants may be applied, again mechanically, for the purpose of ridding the cotton plants of their leaves, thereby hastening the opening of the bolls and expediting mechanical harvesting. When the bolls are open the cotton is harvested. Most farmers in the South Plains employ migratory workers to hand harvest their best cotton and then complete the operation by using mechanical strippers, which strip both open and unopen bolls from the plants and in the process yield a poorer grade of cotton.[20]

Grain sorghum, the other major South Plains crop, is planted somewhat later than cotton, generally in May and early June, though sometimes as late as July. Machinery similar to that employed in cotton growing is used for planting and cultivating grain sorghum. Irrigation both before and after planting is universally practiced, though waterings are less extensive than in the case of cotton. Harvesting is entirely mechanical, involving the use of the combine, or harvester-thresher, for which purpose a dwarf variety of sorghum has been specially bred.

While most South Plains farmers are all-cotton-and-feed farmers, a number of them work vegetables, sesame, and other crops into a rotation system. A still greater number of them use clovers, vetch, and grass crops to build organic matter in their soil and then plant cotton or grain sorghum in a fairly systematic rotation. Such resource processes, however, are only individual variations on the prevailing two-crop cash farming economy of the South Plains.

What, now, are the physical and cultural contexts of these resource processes? How are these contexts related to the development of groundwater as a crucial agricultural resource? By way of answering these questions, let us consider first the set P of resource processes which are possible in the South Plains when this area is viewed as a natural habitat. Following this, we shall consider the set C of socially defined activities (the culture) which is characteristic of the South Plains population. We shall then be in a position to consider groundwater as a natural resource p' which has been "developed" as a result of certain changes in the intersection, or overlap A, of P and C—more precisely, as a result of some new combinations between elements p of P and elements c of C.

The South Plains is distinguished by certain topographical, stratigraphic, and hydrographic characteristics which together make it an easily defined geographic unit.[21] Most of its surface is flat, sloping gently to the east at about six feet per mile. This level surface is spotted with innumerable slight depressions which become ponds after heavy rainstorms. Owing to the impermeable character of the sediments which lie just below the surface, these ponds, ranging in size from a few hundred feet to a mile or so across, sometimes persist for years. Precipitation over the South Plains averages about twenty inches a year, with considerable variation above and below this figure from one year to the next. About three-fourths of the precipitation falls during the growing season, April to September; ninety nine percent of it, however, is lost by evaporation and transpiration. The soils are mostly fine sandy loams and clay loams whose dominant vegetal growth prior to American settlement consisted of short grasses and some shrubs and mesquite.[22]

Underlying the surface of the South Plains, at depths ranging from 150 to 350 feet, is a formation of porous, water bearing sands known as the Ogallala formation. This formation, which is of alluvial origin, ranges in thickness from a fraction of an inch to 400 feet or more and serves as the aquifer for the area's entire supply of fresh water. As a result of surface stream erosion, the Ogallala formation has become hydrologically isolated from surrounding formations, so that percolation of groundwater between it and adjoining regions is impossible. Consequently, withdrawal and natural recharge of groundwater in the South Plains is a wholly autochthonous process.[23]

In the almost utter absence of surface streams, groundwater has become the limiting factor to resource development in the South Plains. In the words of a botanist:

Any hope that great arid regions can be made highly productive without the manipulation of water is most certainly a false hope. Water is too much a key substance in the metabolism of organisms to permit us to suppose for a moment that we can develop masses of vegetation in its absence.[24]

Groundwater, of course, represents just one phase in the hydrologic cycle, but it has important properties which condition its availability as a natural resource. The porosity of the formation in which it is held; the thickness and depth of this formation from the surface; the rate of water flow through its pore spaces; the slope, flora, and temperature at the surface—these and many other physical properties of the South Plains, viewed purely as a natural habitat, go far in determining which physical processes will lie within the set P of possible resource processes.

Of course, not all the elements of P represent adoptable natural resources. Only that subset of P which is formed by the intersection of P with C—the set of socially defined activities, or the culture, of a population—will conform to the range A of adoptable natural resources.[25] In other words, the resource composition of a habitat varies as much with the activities of the people who occupy that habitat— their techniques, beliefs, knowledge, and social organization —as it does with the physical properties of the habitat itself. The truth of this proposition is nowhere more strikingly illustrated than in the South Plains, which as recently as 1900 was described by a geologist as ". . . nonirrigable, either from streams, flowing or stored, or from underground sources, and . . . therefore, for general agriculture, . . . irreclaimable; . . ." [26] What transformation in the culture of the people occupying this area has made "valuable" an element of the habitat which was fully known in 1900 but which was considered then to be "irreclaimable"?

At least three sectors of European and American culture seem to have been decisive in the conversion of certain processes of the South Plains habitat into available natural resources, viz., the technology, the economy, and the polity. We may consider each of these in order.

Undoubtedly, the most conspicuous feature of the South Plains, viewed in terms of the cultural context of its resource processes, is the degree to which those processes involve an industrial technology, a technology based on the mechanized use of inanimate energy. Industrial technology and its adjunct, scientific research, have together converted the physical properties of the South Plains habitat into a productive fund of natural resources. The extent to which South Plains resource processes are mechanized can be seen in the findings of a 1949 sample survey of 100 farmers in Lubbock county, which is situated near the center of the South Plains. Of these 100 farmers, 99 owned tractors, 76 had irrigation wells, 74 owned rotary hoes, 46 owned cotton harvesters and 30 owned combines.[27] Indeed, it has been the tractor, the turbine centrifugal pump for irrigation wells, and the genetic adaptation of cotton and grain sorghum which have figured most prominently in the recent resource development of the South Plains. The significance of these technics lies in the productive efficiency which can be achieved through their use. With modern four-row tractor-mounted equipment, for instance, only 4.30 man hours of work are required to produce an acre of cotton up to the point of harvest. With two-row tractor-mounted equipment the figure is 5.50; with two-row horse-drawn equipment the figure is 6.65; and with one-row horse-drawn equipment it is 10.45.[28] It is not surprising, then, that, with the perfection of the modern tractor and its accompanying equipment, in the 1920's, South Plains resource users shifted rapidly from horse power to tractor power: whereas only 24 per cent of South Plains farmers had tractor power in 1934, 78 per cent of them had it just three years later.[29]

This heavy commitment to mechanized resource processes on the part of South Plains farmers is only the regional correlate of an advanced industrial technology which has become ubiquitous throughout the United States and much of the Western world. As the historian Webb has pointed out, High Plains agriculture was from the beginning predicated on the Industrial Revolution: on railroad transportation, barbed wire fencing, well drilling machinery, refrigeration, and many other technics which have their being, not so much in the High Plains, but in the entire Western world.[30] In this respect, the natural resources of the High Plains are to be viewed as localized variants of a world wide industrial technology which has been joined to the physical features of a particular regional habitat.

The point takes on added force when we look at the two main crops of the South Plains: cotton and grain sorghum. Cotton, as Zimmermann has observed, ". . . is truly the child of the Industrial Revolution." [31] Without power driven machinery and scientific genetics, cotton would not be the principal money-making crop which it has been on the South Plains. To be sure, there are physical features of the South Plains habitat which are just as essential to its cultivation. Cotton requires an abundance of sunshine and a warm temperature before and after its vegetative growth; its germination is affected by a number of soil, water, and temperature variables; its quality is impaired by frost, dust, and untimely rains. In most of these respects, the South Plains offers a favorable habitat for the cotton plant. But without irrigation its cultivation would be (and is) a precarious enterprise indeed. Without genetically adapted strains whose height and maturation have been standardized, there could be no machine harvesting.[32] Without the cotton gin and railroad transportation, too, cotton would not even be part of the resource congeries of the South Plains today—whatever might be the physical properties of this area as a natural habitat. The same is true of grain sorghum. As a plant, grain sorghum is remarkably tolerant of heat and drought, being in this respect well adapted to South Plains climatic conditions. But until plant geneticists had developed varieties which would grow to the height of a combine, or thresher-harvester, thereby permitting mechanical harvesting, the economic value of this crop for South Plains resource users was limited. Since 1957 new hybrid varieties have been perfected which even further enhance the economic value of this crop. These instances further demonstrate the paramount role which industrial technology has played in the conversion of the physical features of a natural habitat into a set of available resource processes. They illustrate the proposition advanced by the historian Malin, that:

The earth possessed all known, and yet to be known, resources, but they were available as natural resources only to a culture that was technically capable of utilizing them.[33]

Technology, of course, does not by itself effect this conversion of inert natural processes into social capital. At least two other sectors of a population's activities are accessory to the phenomenon, viz., the economy and the polity. The organization of a people's production and exchange activities and the character of their political decisions may figure prominently in the very mechanization of their resource processes and can play in their own right a decisive role in the development of a people's natural resources.

Present day resource processes in the South Plains are

quite literally an artifact of the European and American market economy. In such an economy, human agents are governed by the norm of maximizing private gainfulness in their production and exchange activities. The consequences of such a norm, insofar as resource processes are concerned, is a geographic specialization of productive activities; what people do with their land is dictated, not by their subsistence needs, but by what they can get in exchange for their products.

The pre-eminent position which cotton and grain sorghum presently occupy in the South Plains is to be understood in just these terms. Cotton and grain sorghum are not subsistence products; they are export products par excellence. The fact that these two crops alone account for three-fourths of the total income of the South Plains is indicative of the area's involvement in a market economy.[34] Moreover, any significant change in prices for farm products in the future will undoubtedly entail a readjustment in South Plains resource processes as farmers once again seek a most profitable combination of crops. Indeed, the very conversion of the area's one-time ranch lands into farms during the 1920's is attributable to just such a change in price relationships, and it suggests the volatile character of any resource congeries whose composition is dictated by market forces.[35] The processes which today enter into the production of cotton and grain sorghum in the South Plains, and the natural resources which are thereby engendered, clearly owe their origin as much to the apparel and food demands of people the world over, and to alternative sources of supply, as they do to the geographic features of the area as a natural habitat. It is the unstable juxtaposition of elements of the latter with the ever changing elements of a market economy which accounts in large part for the dynamic character of South Plains resource processes, as well as for the continual development of ever new resources in the region.

The market economy, of course, does not operate independently of political decisions. American public land policy, railroad subsidies, freight rate structures, soil conservation programs, and farm price supports have all figured prominently in the development of natural resources in the South Plains. While it would not be accurate to speak of South Plains agriculture as a subsidized agriculture, the metaphor does point up a very real fact, viz., the contingency of South Plains resource processes upon politico-economic decisions that are made in Washington, New York, and other power centers lying wholly outside the region. The question posed in a regional economic survey prepared by the Federal Reserve Bank of Dallas is one which many South Plains resource users have asked of themselves: "Could the area continue to grow cotton profitably if support levels were reduced substantially?" [36] Certainly the present scale of cotton cultivation can not be understood apart from a polity in which decisions concerning farm product prices, acreage allotments, export programs, etc. have played a significant role in determining production opportunities for South Plains resource users. Such decisions must be reckoned among the activities which have been crucial in converting the South Plains habitat into a fund of available natural resources.

There are, of course, still other sectors of the European and American culture, in addition to its technology, its economy, and its polity, which have figured in the development of South Plains natural resources. In all of them we can see the same essential phenomenon: the genesis of a natural resource through the linking of an element or elements p of the set P of physically possible resource processes with certain elements c of the set C of socially defined activities. In this linking there is a transformation of inert natural processes into social capital, affording thereby an increase in the magnitudes of such attributes of a population's activities as their wealth, their power, and their prestige.

What can we say, now, concerning the conditions—the formally necessary conditions—for the development of a natural resource? Is there any general proposition which we can assert, and to which some credibility will attach, that specifies a situation which is invariably present when an inert natural process gets transformed into a natural resource? The substance of such a proposition has been stated in our preceding chapter (Chapter VI). There we had occasion to observe that when factors external to a resource complex change beyond a critical magnitude, an altogether different entity results, one which is highly receptive to new resource processes. These new processes may literally reconstitute the land itself and can endow it with new natural resources. The *causa causans* in this whole transformation lies, not in any single, isolable factor, but rather in the entire set of factors, which are external to a given set of resource processes.[37]

More precisely, for any set A of adoptable resource processes (and hence for the proper subset X of A) there is an "environment" of other resource processes which is constituted by the two sets P and C—the physically possible and the socially defined processes, respectively. This environment may be a stable one or it may be an unstable one. That of twelfth century England was stable, and in it there was no development whatever of new natural resources. The environment of eighteenth century England, on the other hand, was an unstable one; in it, the root crops and artificial grasses were introduced, and through these innovations the supply of winter feed and hence of animals was increased, the effect being an improvement in the fertility and the productive capacity of the very land itself. In the case of the South Plains, the environment represented by P and C has been an unstable one ever since the area's first settlement by American farmers; climatic vicissitudes, new inventions, market trends, labor supply problems, and governmental policies have all lent a volatile aspect to resource processes in the area. The corollary of this has been a conversion of "desert" soils and "irreclaimable" water into a fund of natural resources.

These considerations suggest a formal hypothesis concerning one of the necessary conditions for the development of a natural resource. We may begin by defining a set π of resource processes, each element of which has the characteristic of being outside the set P of possible resource processes at certain periods (or a single period) of time and being inside the set P at other periods (or period) of time. Similarly we may define a set γ of resource processes, each element of which has the characteristic of being outside the set C of socially defined activities at certain periods (or a single period) of time and being inside the set C at other periods (or period) of time. These two sets π and γ may be

taken to designate aspects of instability in the corresponding sets P and C. The sets $-\pi$ and $-\gamma$, relative to P and C,
will be taken to designate the stable features of a physical
and cultural environment. The absence of any elements
whatever in π and γ would, of course, denote complete
stability in P and C. Finally, we may recall our previously
defined set α of resource processes, each element of which
has the characteristic of being outside the set A of adoptable processes at a point in time which is prior to or concurrent with π and/or γ, and being inside the set A at a
specified later point in time. The absence of any elements
in α would denote a state of affairs in which there had been
no development of natural resources during the interval
between the two specified points in time.

The existence of nonempty sets π and γ of resource processes corresponds to the fact of some change, beyond a
critical magnitude, in the "environment" which is external
to a resource system X. Similarly the existence of a nonempty set α of resource processes corresponds to the fact of
resource development, whereby new processes have become
available to a resource system X. From the point of view
of resource users, the two nonempty sets π and γ represent
stimulus situations which, by virtue of their novelty relative
to a prior state of affairs, give rise to a sequence of exploratory, trial-and-error responses on the part of resource users.
In this exploratory behavior, some elements $p \ \varepsilon \ P$ and $c \ \varepsilon \ C$
come to be experimentally combined and recombined with
one another and with various other processes until they
eventually yield two classes of new elements: (1) those
which lie outside the set A and are therefore not adoptable,
and (2) those which lie inside the set A and are therefore

adoptable. The latter class of elements may be called natural resources; or, more accurately, it is the *physical processes,* to which appropriate cultural activities have been linked, that may be called natural resources. They are distinguished from the elements which lie outside of A by their compatibility with a population's system of activities and with the organic and physical possibilities of a habitat. The entire course of events which begins with the existence of elements in the set π or in the set γ of resource processes, and which ends with the discovery of an element $p' \; \varepsilon \; \alpha$, may be called *the development of a natural resource.*

In a summary statement, then, the hypothesis may be advanced that:

$$[\alpha \neq 0] \supset [(\pi \lor \gamma) \neq 0],$$

this being understood as a universally quantified proposition. According to this hypothesis, a necessary condition for the existence of a set of newly developed natural resources is the concurrent or antecedent existence of instability in the set P or the set C of physically possible and socially defined processes, respectively.[38] By virtue of this instability there is a succession of changes in the boundaries of P and C which presents to resource users the opportunity of making new combinations between elements p of P and elements c of C. Some of these combinations fall within the set α, becoming thereby adoptable resource processes. Any physical process which has been thus transformed becomes an adoptable natural resource. From $p \; \varepsilon \; -A$ it has become $p' \; \varepsilon \; \alpha$.

There is, of course, the special case in which a resource process $p \; \varepsilon \; -A$ becomes $p' \; \varepsilon \; X,$ constituting thus an employed natural resource. This phenomenon, however, does not differ in any essential respect from the more general case. What distinguishes it is simply the fact that the new resource process is situated not only within the set A of adoptable resource processes but also within the subset $(G \lor L) < A$ of gainful and/or likely resource processes.[39] The causation of the phenomenon, however, is in every respect identical with that of the more general case. Indeed, as we shall presently see, the development of a natural resource is never an abrupt, *einmalig* event which can be precisely dated but is rather a continuing course of events, during which the efficiency and the likelihood of a new process may be very uncertain quantities from one time to another.

We now have a hypothesis before us which states a necessary, though not a necessary and sufficient, condition for the development of a natural resource. Proof of the hypothesis would require our specifying a comprehensive sample of resource complexes and congeries and then establishing the fact that in this sample there was no case in which the antecedent, $\alpha \neq 0$, was present and in which the consequent, $(\pi \lor \gamma) \neq 0$, was absent. No such proof has been attempted in the present study. Instead, we have limited ourselves to the task of illustrating our hypothesis with a single case, that of groundwater development in the South Plains—a procedure which admittedly can do no more than impart some plausibility to our hypothesis. Yet the enterprise should be by no means a fruitless one.

The existence of groundwater in the South Plains seems to have been known to the earliest settlers.[40] Its abundant supply had been surmised by many. Only its great depth from the surface precluded its immediate availability as a natural resource. During the 1880's, however, ranchers found themselves driven to seek more dependable and ample sources of water for their stock than that which was available in the few streams and springs. Dug wells, and bored wells, too, were out of the question because of the depth of the water-bearing formation from the surface. Drilling equipment was accordingly imported and water wells were put into operation as early as 1887. Most of these early wells were pumped by windmills, though in some instances they were pumped by horse power.[41]

In the meantime, agriculturists were beginning to settle in the South Plains. Their activities were immediately conditioned by what is the outstanding aspect of instability in the South Plains habitat: limited and uncertain rainfall. The years 1883-85, for instance, were years of unusually good rainfall; those of 1891-93, on the other hand, were drought years.[42] Subsequent experience and research has shown that, while the mean annual precipitation for the South Plains is 15 inches during the growing season, the year-to-year departures from this average are exceedingly great.[43] Water requirements for the two principal crops of the area, cotton and grain sorghum, range between 24 and 39 inches for the growing season. Yet, on the basis of past experience, farmers can expect to have 20 or more inches of rainfall in a single growing season only ten percent of the time. The probability of adequate rainfall in any one growing season is thus exceedingly small.[44]

Such uncertainty in the water supply naturally provoked a great deal of speculation and experimentation on the part of early South Plains farmers. At the turn of the century proposals were already being made for irrigating the land by pumping groundwater to the surface. But skepticism as to the feasibility of irrigation was widespread.[45] Windmills could at best irrigate no more than four acres of land.[46] Hence attention quickly shifted to the possibility of motor driven pumps. As early as 1904 there was speculation about the use of gasoline engines as a source of power; steam engines were actually tried but were found to be prohibitively expensive in their operation.[47]

With the extension of a railroad to Lubbock in 1909, a new era of agricultural development began. For the first time, crops could be shipped to distant markets. Land values accordingly rose, and a renewed interest in the possibilities of irrigation developed. In 1910, a delegation of Plainview business men went to Portales, New Mexico to inspect irrigation experiments that were under way in that area. Upon their return they entered into arrangements with a local farmer to drill a test well on his place. A 130-foot well was drilled, and a centrifugal pump, powered with a tractor, was used to lift the water to the surface.[48] The well proved to be productive.

Following this initial success, additional wells were drilled, despite the doubts of most farmers that there would be enough groundwater to provide for sustained irrigation development. By 1914, more than 100 wells had been drilled and put into operation. But a series of years of generally good rainfall between 1919 and 1925 took much of the momentum out of this initial groundwater development. Moreover, the pumps in these early wells, powered as they were with large, oil-burning engines, proved to be prohibitively expensive to install and operate. It is not surprising, then, that during the entire quarter century following the first motorized well of 1911, only 600 irrigation wells were drilled in the Texas South Plains.[49]

In the meantime, however, the relative market opportunities for cotton and cattle were undergoing a pronounced change. Relatively high cotton prices, alongside sharply declining cattle prices, led to a breaking up of the ranches and a rapid conversion of land from cattle to cotton. The 1920's were years of unprecedented agricultural expansion in the South Plains. Land values rose, tractor power displaced horse power, and farm population increased. Then, beginning in 1927 and intensifying after 1933, a profound drought struck the area, a drought which was not relieved until 1941 except for brief respites in 1928, 1930, 1932, and 1937. Once again farmers turned to groundwater.

It was not until the middle of the 1930's, however, that a major technological breakthrough was achieved which, with the climatic and price factors already noted, led to full-scale development of groundwater as an employed natural resource. In 1935 or 1936, the high-speed automobile engine, with its direct drive, was combined with the high-speed, turbine centrifugal pump, and a veritable revolution in South Plains resource processes took place. The combination of these two technics yielded a motorized pumping unit which for the first time made deep well irrigation a practicable resource process.[50] Meanwhile additional sources of power were becoming available. Electric power transmission lines were extended into the South Plains and led to some adoption of electric motors as power units. But by the 1950's, butane and natural gas had come to be the principal fuels for the automotive and industrial engines which now powered most of the irrigation pumps on the South Plains.[51]

Between 1936 and World War II, farmers throughout the South Plains were engaged in an ambitious program of well drilling. Nearly 1,100 wells were completed during the three years 1937 to 1939. Then, with the war and its accompanying shortages of materials, well drilling was temporarily curtailed. Two successive years of abundant rainfall, in 1941 and 1942, removed some of the incentive, too, for installing irrigation wells. But by this time another unsettling feature of the South Plains cultural "environment" had come into play. This was the federal program of agricultural price supports, effected through acreage allotments and marketing quotas, and designed to give American farmers "parity," relative to city people, in the prices received for their products. As a result of this governmental policy, cotton prices rose, after a low in 1939, to unprecedented levels during the late 1940's and the 1950's. South Plains farmers again turned to groundwater. Experience had taught them that yields on irrigated farms were nearly double those on unirrigated "dryland" farms. Attracted by high prices for their principal crop, cotton, farmers now looked to irrigation, not only as an insurance against drought, but as a means of increasing their yields and thereby their profits.[52] Groundwater forthwith became converted at an unprecedented rate into an employed natural resource. By 1948, there were 8,346 wells in operation in the 43 counties comprising the Texas portion of the South Plains; three years later, in 1951, there were 16,509 wells; by 1954 there were 27,983 wells; and by 1957 there were 42,225 wells. The number of acres irrigated by these wells, for the corresponding years, was as follows: in 1948, 1,159,600 acres; in 1951, 2,230,965 acres; in 1954, 3,627,105 acres; and in 1957, 4,568,880 acres.[53] In short, ". . . since 1943 the expansion of irrigation in the High Plains has been spectacular."[54]

In this succession of challenges and responses, we have the essential dynamics of resource development. South Plains resource users have been from the beginning confronted with factors of instability in their physical and cultural environments: unpredictably good rainfall followed by drought; widely fluctuating prices for farm products; technological innovations in well drilling, irrigation pumps and power units; federal acreage controls and marketing quotas, etc. These factors of instability, comprising elements in the sets π and γ, respectively, represent stimuli in what is essentially a perceptual learning situation.[55] They are a necessary, though not a necessary and sufficient, condition for the development of any natural resource. Just as in all perceptual learning, the particular combination p and c which yields the natural resource p' is the outcome of a long process of exploratory behavior in which many other combinations, among the changing elements of P and C, have been attempted and found wanting (i.e., have fallen within the set $-A$). Of the combinations p and c which do yield natural resources, some are put to actual use as social capital while others remain unused, representing only potential social capital. Both, however, constitute natural resources.

The question now arises of determining the conditions under which a natural resource, once developed, is put to actual use. What circumstances invariably attend a population's employment of a natural resource as social capital? More precisely, what are the necessary conditions under which a particular p' becomes an element of the resource congeries X'' ($< A$) and perhaps of the resource complex X' ($< X'' < A$)?

NOTES

1. Derwent Whittlesey, "Sequent Occupance," *Annals of the Association of American Geographers*, XIX (1929), 162-65.

2. Anthony Scott, *Natural Resources: the Economics of Conservation* (Toronto: University of Toronto Press, 1955), p. 3.

3. The following analysis has in large part been inspired by the functional theory of resources which is developed by Erich W. Zimmermann in his *World Resources and Industries* (rev. ed.; New York: Harper and Bros., 1951), esp. chaps. i-iii, vii-ix.

4. Cf. *ibid.*, chap. i.

5. Cf. the compatible definitions of conservation advanced in S. V. Ciriacy-Wantrup, *Resource Conservation* (Berkeley and Los Angeles: University of California Press, 1952), p. 51; and in Scott, *op. cit.*, p. 18.

6. A term applied originally by Robert Trow-Smith to recent British agricultural processes. See his *English Husbandry* (London: Faber and Faber Ltd., 1951), p. 186.

7. Norman Scott Brien Gras, *A History of Agriculture in Europe and America* (New York: F. S. Crofts Co., 1925), p. 356.

8. For a comprehensive characterization of the American Great Plains and its history, see the classic work of Walter Prescott Webb, *The Great Plains* (Boston: Ginn and Co., 1931).

9. Frances Phillips, *The Development of Agriculture in the Panhandle-Plains Region of Texas to 1920,* Unpublished Master's thesis, West Texas State Teachers College, 1946, p. 9.

10. *Ibid.*, pp. 43, 62.

11. *Ibid.*, pp. 24-25.

12. *Ibid.*, pp. 41-42, 49-51.

13. *Ibid.*, pp. 70-74.

14. Ernest C. Ratliff, *A Survey, Analytical and Historical, of Irrigation*

in Hale County, Texas, Unpublished Master's thesis, Texas Technological College, 1938, pp. 17-20.

15. This second wave of settlers has remained somewhat distinct from previous settlers in regard to social status, attitudes toward farming, and several other respects. See: Wilfrid C. Bailey, "The Status System of a Texas Panhandle Community," *Texas Journal of Science,* V (1953), 326-31.

16. Phillips, *op. cit.,* p. 65.

17. *Ibid.,* p. 75.

18. A. C. Magee, C. A. Bonnen, and B. H. Thibodeaux, *Information Basic to Farm Adjustments in the High Plains Cotton Area of Texas* (Texas Agricultural Experiment Station Research Bulletin 652 [College Station, 1944]), pp. 50-52.

19. William F. Hughes and Joe R. Motheral, *Irrigated Agriculture in Texas* (Texas Agricultural Experiment Station Miscellaneous Publication 59 [College Station, 1950]), p. 17.

20. A detailed description of the technology of South Plains cotton production is presented in H. P. Smith and D. L. Jones, *Mechanized Production of Cotton in Texas* (Texas Agricultural Experiment Station Research Bulletin 704 [College Station, 1948]). For a history of the mechanization of cotton production, see James H. Street, *The New Revolution in the Cotton Economy* (Chapel Hill, N. C.: University of North Carolina Press, 1957), chaps. v-viii. On the socio-economic correlates of farm mechanization in the southwest, see Alvin L. Bertrand, J. L. Charlton, Harald A. Pedersen, R. L. Skrabanek, and James D. Tarver, *Factors Associated with Agricultural Mechanization in the Southwest Region* (Arkansas Agricultural Experiment Station Research Bulletin 567 [Fayetteville, 1956]).

21. See esp. J. R. Barnes, W. C. Ellis, E. R. Leggat, R. A. Scalapino, and W. O. George, *Geology and Ground Water in the Irrigated Region of the Southern High Plains in Texas* (Texas Board of Water Engineers, Progress Report No. 7 [Austin, 1949]), pp. 6-27.

22. Magee, Bonnen and Thibodeaux, *op. cit.*

23. W. N. White, W. L. Broadhurst, and J. W. Lang, *Ground Water in the High Plains of Texas* (U. S. Geological Survey Water Supply Paper 889-F [Washington, D. C., 1946]), pp. 385-86; Barnes *et al., op. cit.,* pp. 12-13.

24. W. Gordon Whaley, "Arid Lands and Plant Research," *Scientific Monthly,* LXXV (1952), 228-33.

25. Cf. Zimmermann, *op. cit.,* p. 13, diagram.

26. Willard D. Johnson, "The High Plains and Their Utilization," *Twenty-first Annual Report, United States Geological Survey,* Part IV: "Hydrology" (Washington, D. C.: U. S. Government Printing Office, 1901), p. 611.

27. Leon R. Tabor, *Services Used by Farmers in Lubbock County,*

Texas, Unpublished Master's thesis, Texas Technological College, 1950.

28. Magee, Bonnen, and Thibodeaux, *op. cit.,* pp. 16-18.

29. *Ibid.,* p. 52; Street, *op. cit.,* p. 95.

30. Webb, *op. cit.,* pp. 271-72, 333; Zimmermann, *op. cit.,* chap. x.

31. Zimmermann, *op. cit.,* p. 325.

32. *Ibid.,* p. 333. The agricultural experiment station at Lubbock, operating since 1909, has exerted wide influence on crops and farming methods throughout the South Plains.

33. James C. Malin, "Ecology and History," *Scientific Monthly,* LXX (1950), 296.

34. Specifically, in 1949 they accounted for 83 per cent of the area's total income. *Economic and Banking Problems of the Lubbock Area* (Depbartment of Research, Federal Reserve Bank of Dallas), June, 1950, p. 15.

35. On price instability as a generalized characteristic of American agriculture, see Theodore W. Schultz, *The Economic Organization of Agriculture* (New York: McGraw-Hill Book Co., 1953), p. 337.

36. *Economic and Banking Problems . . . ,* p, 21.

37. On this conception of social causation see particularly: Pitirim A. Sorokin, *Social and Cultural Dynamics* (New York: American Book Co., 1941), Vol. IV, chaps. xii-xiv; Sorokin, *Society, Culture, and Personality* (New York: Harper and Bros., 1947), chaps. xliii, xlvi; Talcott Parsons, *The Social System* (Glencoe, Ill.: The Free Press, 1951), chap. xi.

38. The asserted truth of this hypothesis is synthetic rather than tautological, inasmuch as nothing in our specification of set relations as between A (of which p' is an element), and π and γ, would logically compel it. The elements of $\pi \vee \gamma$ *need* not be elements of A, nor vice versa.

39. This is a matter which is going to engage us in Chapter VIII.

40. Willard D. Johnson, "The High Plains and their Utilization," *Twenty-second Annual Report, United States Geological Survey,* Part IV: "Hydrology" (Washington: U. S. Government Printing Office, 1902), pp. 640ff.

41. Riley E. Baker, "Water Development as an Important Factor in the Utilization of the High Plains of Texas," *Southwestern Social Science Quarterly,* XXXIV (1953), 21-34, citing J. Evetts Haley, *The XIT Ranch of Texas and the Early Days of the Llano Estacado* (Chicago: Lakeside Press, 1929), p. 94. See Baker, p. 23. These facts, and much of the account which follows, are based on Baker's analysis and interpretation of water development on the South Plains.

42. Baker, *ibid.,* p. 27.

43. Barnes, Ellis, *et al., op. cit.,* p. 15.

44. Edwin Lincoln Harrington, *A Study of Some Factors Affecting the Efficient Use of Irrigation Water in Texas,* Unpublished Ph.D. dissertation, Agricultural and Mechanical College of Texas, 1952, p. 53.

45. For examples of these respective opinions, see Phillips, *op. cit.*, pp. 90-91.

46. Baker, *op. cit.*, p. 29.

47. Phillips, *op. cit.*, pp. 91-95.

48. Baker, *op. cit.*; Ratliff, *op. cit.*, pp. 17-18; see also the *Plainview Sunday Herald*, September 18, 1955.

49. W. L. Broadhurst, *Ground-Water in the High Plains of Texas* (Texas Board of Water Engineers, Progress Report No. 6 [Austin, January, 1947]); Baker, *op. cit.*, p. 32.

50. *Ibid.*, p. 33.

51. *Ibid.*, pp. 33-34.

52. Charles Benjamin Brotherton, *The Economics of Shallow-Water Irrigation in the Texas High Plains*, Unpublished Master's thesis, Agricultural and Mechanical College of Texas, 1948, p. 23.

53. *Lubbock Avalanche-Journal*, July 14, 1957.

54. Barnes, Ellis, *et al.*, *op. cit.*, p. 28.

55. Cf. Zimmermann, *op. cit.*, p. 36.

CHAPTER VIII

THE USE
OF NATURAL RESOURCES

'Till jarring interests, of themselves
create
Th' according music of a well-
mixed state.

ALEXANDER POPE *

$\mathcal{A}$ RESOURCE is being used only when it is put to a purpose. Since most resources can be put to a variety of purposes, they admit of a number of uses. Yet not all of these uses are compatible with one another. Hence, the first task of the resource planner must be one of distinguishing good from bad uses relative to a variety of purposes. To give consistency to his decisions the planner needs a theory which will yield precepts telling him under what conditions one or another resource use is good or bad. It is just such a theory that we have been looking for. Our assumption all along has been that any attribute, or combination of attributes, which is universally characteristic of systems of resource processes must in some sense be a necessary one, and is therefore a good one. Such a property, we have assumed, can be taken as an existential element in rational resource planning and policy making.

Thus far, our study has given a prominent place to two particular attributes of resource processes. These are the attributes of gainfulness (which is a subjective correlate of economic efficiency) and likelihood (which is a subjective correlate of interpersonal predictability). They may be designated, respectively, as G, $-G$ and L, $-L$, the two components of each being "magnitudes" into which both of the attributes can be dichotomized.[1] With respect to these attributes, our study has suggested that the resource user is governed by two incentives: first, by the incentive to employ additional processes which will be gainful to him in respect to economic efficiency, and second, by the incentive to employ additional processes which are generally observed in his social order and to which he expects to be held accountable. The first of these incentives leads to a choice of G in preference to $-G$; the second leads to a choice of L in preference to $-L$.

In our analysis of cases, we have been led to believe that the two magnitudes G and L stand in a somewhat equivocal relationship to one another. We have also been led to believe that the attributes G, $-G$ and L, $-L$ in a resource system have their magnitudes affected by the stability or instability of the larger physical and cultural environment. Can we, now, anticipate a theory that will state both of these propositions as postulates from which true theorems about resource use may be inferred? If we can do this, and if the two propositions are indeed universally true, we might regard such a theory as a verified or unfalsified one.[2] Furthermore, any theorem which is then stateable in terms of the theory may be properly taken as a precept for rational planning and policy making.

With this general objective in mind, let us turn to our immediate problem. Our analysis of groundwater development in the southern High Plains, as set forth in the preceding chapter, has pointed to one of the conditions under which a natural resource becomes developed and adoptable. Our present task, now, consists of establishing the conditions which are necessary for the actual use of an adoptable resource. We shall approach the problem by first listing all the types of resource processes that are logically possible in terms of the two dichotomous attributes of gainfulness and likelihood. Then, with this list before us, we shall try to determine which of these conceivable types are in fact represented in the cases that have been described in our study. Finally, on the basis of these empirically realized types, we shall attempt to state a general theory which will specify the formal conditions under which adoptable resource processes are put to use.

The logically possible combinations of distinct pairs of the components of $G,\ -G$ *and* $L,\ -L$ are, of course, four in number. They consist of: (1) processes which are both gainful and likely ($G \cdot L$); (2) processes which are nongainful and likely ($-G \cdot L$); (3) processes which are gainful and nonlikely ($G \cdot -L$); and (4) processes which are nongainful and nonlikely ($-G \cdot -L$). This list exhausts all the types (empirically nonempty subsets) of resource processes that are conceivable in terms of the two dichotomous attributes of gainfulness and likelihod. Hence, any employed resource process, out of a set A of adoptable resource processes, is bound to lie in one or another of these four types. Which of them, now, do in fact include employed resource processes? Are *employed* natural resources, as distinct from *available* natural resources, characterized by certain combinations of the components of G, $-G$ and L, $-L$ and not by others?

Our answer to this question has already been anticipated. In our previous account of English open field agriculture, we were led to the formulation of two hypotheses concerning the composition, first, of a resource complex, and second, of a resource congeries. According to the first hypothesis, every resource complex is comprised of processes which fall within just two combinations of the components of G, $-G$ and L, $-L$, viz.:

$$(G \cdot L) \vee (-G \cdot L).$$

According to the second hypothesis, every resource congeries is comprised of processes which fall within three combinations of the components of G, $-G$ and L, $-L$, viz.:

$$(G \cdot L) \vee (-G \cdot L) \vee (G \cdot -L).$$

Both of these hypotheses represent empirical restrictions on the range of logically possible types, or subsets, of resource processes. The combination $(-G \cdot -L)$ is not present in either a resource complex or a resource congeries; the combination $(G \cdot -L)$ is not present in a resource complex. Hence, by these hypotheses, elements of a set A of adoptable resource processes which fall within the first of the excluded combinations will not be put to use as social capital but will remain only as available natural resources; elements which fall within the second of the excluded combinations will be put to use only under special conditions.

Both of these hypotheses concerning the composition of employed resource processes may be further documented by data on the southern High Plains. In our last chapter we outlined the development of South Plains groundwater from an inert natural process into potential capital and then, with the adaptation of the internal combustion engine to the turbine centrifugal pump, into actual capital. In this latter phase, groundwater has become an element of the set X'', specifically of a resource congeries. A set of available resource processes has thus become a set of employed resource processes. Let us now observe how these employed resource processes are distributed with respect to the four logically possible types of resource processes. In this discussion we shall limit ourselves to the Texas portion of the South Plains, inasmuch as constitutional and statutory factors have led to certain differences between Texas and New Mexico in respect to their irrigation development.

At the outset, it is clear that irrigation per se has become a gainful practice for most South Plains resource users. Moreover, it accords fully with their expectations of one another's behavior. It is, therefore, both gainful and likely. Actual calculation of the productive efficiency of various factor combinations for South Plains farms is exceedingly difficult, owing to the number of variable factors involved: various soil types, cropping systems, crop prices, overhead costs, yield rates of wells, types of power units, types of fuels, etc.[3] However, crop yields on irrigated farms are about double those on dryland farms, and they are far more certain. The magnitude of this yield differential alone is more than enough to compensate for the costs which farmers incur in installing and operating their irrigation equipment. Prior to present day power units and pumps, to be sure, irrigation was not a gainful practice. In 1915, when oil-burning engines were the main source of power, the average cost of irrigation per acre-foot of water was five hundred dollars; by 1947, when inexpensive natural gas, butane and electricity as sources of power became available, it had become less than ten dollars.[4] This phenomenal reduction in pumping costs, made possible by technological improvements, has been the overriding factor in putting irrigation into the category of gainful resource processes.

Moreover, irrigation has come to be the expected, the likely practice in South Plains agriculture. It has not always been so. Farmers who settled the South Plains prior to the mid-1920's, before the last of the ranches had been broken up, were characterized by a somewhat fatalistic, passive attitude toward nature which made them skeptical of the possibilities of irrigation. Newer settlers—those arriving after the final breakup of the ranches—have shown a more rational, active attitude toward nature which has made them highly receptive to new agricultural techniques.[5] To them, irrigation is an available productive technique which can and should be put to use. Its place in their thinking can be gauged from the following account of a recently developed portion of the South Plains:

Water-well digging has become a primary topic of conversation recently. Everyone is interested in what the other fellow is doing water-wellwise. "If John Doe can get water out of that ground, then I can too," that's the impression of some farmers. Each new digging operation gets minute attention from neighbors near and far.[6]

The use of groundwater for irrigation farming, then, may be classed as a gainful and likely practice. As such, it is an employed resource process which can be located within the combination $G \cdot L$ in our list of logically possible types of resource processes.

There are some respects, however, in which South Plains resource users have been engaged in irrigation practices that are gainful but not likely. This class of practices may be broadly characterized by the term "waste." The criterion of waste, in this instance, is not economic efficiency, but rather some normative standard of wise use. The sense in which such practices are gainful but not likely may be seen in the disposition of runoff water. A good many farms in the South Plains have just enough slope to their surface that irrigation water, as it flows down the furrows, will accumulate in stagnant pools at low lying points in the fields. Frequently it will overflow the boundaries of one farm and flood portions of neighbors' farms, as well as roadways and even townsites. An offending farmer, of course, is eager to clear his fields of the excess water in order to prevent damage to his crops. His neighbors, however, are just as eager to keep his runoff water from flooding their fields and damaging their crops. Resource users have sometimes been driven to constructing levees in an effort to keep someone else's water from ruining their crops. From the offender's point of view, the practice is a gainful one, just as the pillaging of forests and the mining of topsoil have been gainful practices for resource users in other parts of the country; for a particular operator working in a limited time span, it represents a least cost combination of productive factors. At the same time, though, it is contrary to the phenomenal expectations which resource users have of one another. It is not the kind of behavior that they expect of their fellows.

Runoff water is only the most visible manifestation of waste. In a number of other ways South Plains resource users have been extravagant with their groundwater resources. Many farmers apply water to their fields far in excess of crop requirements. Others apply water too frequently. Open ditches, so ubiquitous throughout the South Plains, account for substantial water losses through seepage and evaporation. Some farmers have begun planting vegetables and other produce crops that are new to the area— crops whose water requirements are high relative to cotton and grain sorghum—and thus present their neighbors with the problem of doing likewise or of risking their fair "take" of a limited supply of groundwater. These practices, however wasteful they might seem by certain canons of wise use, are at times quite profitable. They are, that is to say, gainful. Yet the injury, real or fanciful, which they impose on other resource users renders them nonlikely in the expectations of the general population. Such practices may therefore be located within the combination $G \cdot -L$ in our fourfold classification of resource processes. It will be recalled, incidentally, that this type of resource process is the distinguishing characteristic of a resource congeries and is not found in a resource complex.

Another class of resource processes which is represented in the South Plains is comprised of those processes which are nongainful and likely. Common to such processes is an awareness, on the part of the resource user, of the probable reactions of other resource users to his own behavior, and a concern on his part to have those reactions comport with

his long run security rather than with his immediate gainfulness. Certain conservation measures, notably the optimum spacing of wells, the installation of recharge wells,
and (in some respects) the use of underground pipe and
closed distribution facilities rather than open ditches, all
illustrate this type of resource process. The clearest example
is the first of these. In the past there was some tendency
on the part of South Plains farmers to locate their new wells
near the older proven wells of neighbors, partly to benefit
from the same advantages of terrain and accessibility, and
partly to ensure that the new wells would at least be productive. The result of this practice was a clustering of wells
at favored sites. Sharp drawdowns in water level resulted
which sometimes impaired the water yields of neighbors'
wells and gave rise to misunderstanding and resentment
among the farmers affected. As the problem came to be
recognized, there evolved an understanding among many
farmers that new wells should be drilled at a sufficient distance from neighbors' wells so that mutual interference in
water yields would not result. In the last few years, this
voluntary spacing of wells has been given legal implemen-
tation by a locally drafted regulatory statute—a development which we shall discuss in fuller detail at another
place. Well spacing has come to be an expected practice
over most of the South Plains today, even though it is
frequently to the economic disadvantage of some individual
resource users. The motivation for it derives from the long
run stake which every resource user has in the spacing of
his own and his neighbors' water wells and hence his felt
accountability to behave as he expects them to behave.
There is thus an aspect of constraint in his behavior, an

aspect which is characteristic of resource processes that fall within the combination $-G \cdot L$ of our typology of resource processes.

The fourth and last type of resource process in our list of logically possible combinations of the components of G, $-G$ and L, $-L$ is that represented by the subset $-G \cdot -L$—the nongainful and the nonlikely. This type, according to our two hypotheses, should not be expected in any system of resource processes. Our supposition seems to be confirmed by the South Plains case. Any number of resource processes are technically available to South Plains farmers which have not been put to actual use, for the reason that they are neither gainful nor likely. Some of these processes, indeed, have had their active proponents. Among them are the following: rationing the pumping of groundwater on a pro rata basis among irrigation farmers (locally known as "proration"); restricting the drilling of new irrigation wells; limiting the acreage that may be irrigated per well; modifying landowners' fee simple title to groundwater; etc. More drastic proposals include the retiring of land from agricultural production and its reversion to pasture and ranching; the piping of surface water from the Mississippi river to the High Plains; subsidizing large scale artificial rain making; etc. None of these available resource processes is either economically or politically feasible at the present time. Accordingly, they have not been employed, however adoptable they might be from a technical or engineering point of view.

Employed resource processes, then, as distinct from available resource processes, seem to be characterized by certain combinations of the components of G, $-G$ and L, $-L$ and not by others. In this respect, the South Plains case reinforces the conclusions which we drew from our analysis of English open field agriculture. The combination $-G \cdot -L$ is found in neither of these systems of resource processes, and the combination $G \cdot -L$ is found only in such resource congeries as post-1700 English agriculture, and contemporary South Plains agriculture. Can we take these findings, now, and do anything further with them? Can we so relate them to a general theory of resource use that they become logically consistent with other known facts and predictive of still further facts which are as yet unknown? In short, can we "explain" the empirical restrictions which we have found to apply to the types of resource processes that are logically possible?

At the outset it appears that, in the resource systems which we have been describing, there is some value which attaches to every available resource process. By "value" is to be understood ". . . a preference which is felt and/or considered to be justified—'morally' or by reasoning or by aesthetic judgments, . . ." [7] Different resource processes, of course, will not be equally valued. More than this, however, they will not all fall on a single scale or dimension of valuation, from the point of view of the resource user.[8] That is to say, resource users are not able to take any and every pair of resource processes and say that one is superior (or equal) to the other on a scale of valuation. To be sure, processes which are both gainful and likely are presumably valued more than those which are neither gainful nor likely. Processes which are gainful and nonlikely, and processes which are nongainful and likely, seem to stand in an intermediate position between the first two of these types.

But between themselves, gainful and nonlikely processes, on the one hand, and nongainful and likely processes, on the other hand, are not comparable on a scale of valuation. For instance, the perfunctory disposal from one's own fields of runoff water, to the possible detriment of one's neighbor's crops, may be more gainful for an individual than the optimum spacing of wells, but it is at the same time less likely in people's expectations. The two processes, therefore, cannot be ranked on a single dimension of valuation but must rather be viewed as incomparable with respect to value. Hence, the relationship between the four logically possible types of resource processes, viewed as combinations of the components of G, $-G$ and L, $-L$, is only a partial order rather than a simple or complete order. It may be diagrammed as follows:

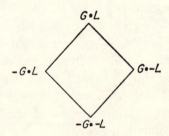

Figure 3.

In this representation, a resource process which falls within the subset $G \cdot L$ will be valued more than one falling within any of the other three types; hence, it may be placed at the top of the diagram. A resource process which falls within either $G \cdot -L$ or $-G \cdot L$ will be valued more than one falling within $-G \cdot -L;$ these combinations may accordingly be placed above the latter on the diagram. But a resource process which falls within $G \cdot -L$ cannot be considered more valued than one which falls within $-G \cdot L;$ the two processes are simply incomparable and hence, they are to be placed in a horizontal position without any connecting line between them. The diagram as a whole represents a "domain of positions" in which the "type-parts" are alternative combinations of magnitudes of gainfulness and likelihood.[9]

It will be noted that in this diagram we have defined an inverted image, or dual, of the system of subsets which was defined in the equation on page 105 of Chapter V. That is to say, where $G \cdot L$ appears in that equation as a minimal subset, it appears as a maximal subset in Figure 3. The permutation which has thus been effected corresponds to the fact that, in the first instance the four subsets or types of resource processes are arranged according to the presumed number of processes that are included in each of them, whereas in the present instance the four subsets or types are arranged according to the worth or value which resource users are presumed to attach to each of them. Thus, the subset $G \cdot L$ is minimal with respect to the first ordering and is maximal with respect to the second ordering. The legitimacy of such a permutation is, of course, an empirical question which can only be judged by the consequences, for scientific prediction, which follow from it. An important logical consequence of the permutation, however, is a replacement of the operation of union ($\lor$), applying to different subsets or types, by the operation of intersection ($\cdot$).

Now, insofar as the findings of our case studies warrant

any kind of generalization, it would appear that a necessary condition for the employment of a resource process is that it lie *above* the subset $-G \cdot -L$ of resource processes. Inclusion in either $G \cdot -L$ or $-G \cdot L$ seems to be a necessary condition for a resource process' being put to use.[10] With this minimum requirement met, an adoptable process may become an employed process. It thereby becomes an element of a resource system X. From this we may conclude that a newly developed natural resource will only be put to use if it exhibits a minimum magnitude on at least one of two distinct dimensions, either that of gainfulness or that of likelihod. It must be efficient or it must be expected. Otherwise it will remain an unused though available element of the set A of adoptable resource processes.

Taken as an isolated statement, of course, this proposition does not carry us very far in our quest for a general theory of resource use. But by stating a general empirical relationship in terms of a multidimensional attribute of resource processes, it does suggest an interesting parallel between the operations by which resource processes seem to be selected for use, on the one hand, and the formal logical (algebraic) operations which can be performed on the elements of a partially ordered system, on the other hand. Let us look a little further into the nature of this asserted parallel between two orders of fact: the one, empirical, the other, logical. If we can make out a plausible case for a parallel, or correspondence, between a system of empirical operations and a system of logical (algebraic) operations, we shall have gone a long way toward formulating a general theory of resource use. We shall then be able to take the purely formal relationships which hold within our logical system as clues to what we will find in our empirical system. In this sense, predictions might be made, the synthetic truth of which would then have to be ascertained. Insofar as the predictions thus inferred were indeed true propositions, the entire fund of empirical propositions that were thus stated, in correspondence with the elements and operations of our logical system, could then be characterized as a true theory of resource processes. Such a theory, we have argued all along, might then serve as a set of precepts for rational resource planning and policy making.

A natural route to constructing such a theory is available in lattice theory—a branch of mathematics which has formalized the algebraic operations that can be performed on the elements of a partially ordered system.[11] For various subsets of resource processes to be properly represented as elements of a lattice we shall have to make an assumption. Before stating this assumption, let us first suppose that data on the relative gainfulness and the relative likelihood of all the resource processes in a set A of adoptable processes are available such that one can view these two attributes as serials of the form $G_a, \ldots, G_j$ and $L_a, \ldots, L_j$, having however no absolute zeros or absolute units.[12] Now, if we are to order such data in lattice theory, we must assume that any two combinations of a magnitude of G with a magnitude of L are together "contained" in another combination of such magnitudes, and also that each of the two combinations "contains" yet another combination of such magnitudes. More specifically, we must assume that any two combinations $G_a \cdot L_j$ and $G_j \cdot L_a$ (where $a < j$) are together "contained" in another combination $G_j \cdot L_j$ and that each of them "contains" another combination $G_a \cdot L_a$, as follows:

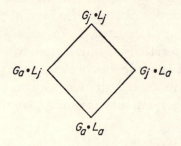

Figure 4.

The empirical counterpart of the term "contain" is the relationship of "valued more than," as explained in our description of Figure 3, on p. 176.

If this is a plausible assumption to make concerning the formal relationship between various combinations of the magnitudes of gainfulness and likelihood, we may properly regard the algebraic operations of lattice theory as paralleling the empirical operations by which resource users select the elements of a set X of employed resource processes out of the elements of a set A of adoptable resource processes.[13] The join or union ($\vee$) and the meet or intersection ($\cdot$) can be taken as counterparts to the operations which resource users perform in perceiving and then evaluating alternative resource processes with a view to putting them to use.[14] Hence, the theorems in a general theory of resource use can be expressed in the form of lattice polynomials—propositions which connect different combinations $G_d \cdot L_e$ and

$G_f \cdot L_g$ ($d, e, f, g \leqslant j$) by means of one or both of the foregoing operations.

Let us now apply these considerations to a specific problem. We have said that inclusion in one of the two subsets $G \cdot -L$ or $-G \cdot L$ is a necessary condition for a resource process' being put to use. We have suggested, too, that the first of these subsets reveals an incentive on the part of resource users to employ additional gainful resource processes. The second of the two subsets, we have suggested, reveals an incentive to employ additional likely processes. In Chapter VI, in the course of our account of the breakdown of open field agriculture, we analyzed rather fully the incentive of resource users to employ additional gainful processes. Let us now enter into a similar analysis of the other incentive, the one which induces resource users to willingly engage in additional processes that are nongainful but likely.

More specifically, let us inquire into the empirical operations by which resource users select for use (from a set A of adoptable resource processes) certain resource processes that are less gainful than, but as likely as, the most valued resource processes? "Why" do resource users employ processes which fall within the subset $G_i \cdot L_j$ (in addition, of course, to processes which fall within $G_j \cdot L_j$), when the elements of $G_i \cdot L_j$ are valued less than the elements of $G_j \cdot L_j$? Let us approach our problem, first in terms of empirical materials, and then, retrospectively, in terms of lattice theory, keeping in mind our assertion that there is supposed to be a correspondence between the two orders of facts.

One of the problems which has characterized South Plains irrigation since its incorporation into the area's resource congeries is that of a declining water table. Natural recharge of the underground water bearing formation is a negligible quantity owing to the low precipitation and high evaporation rates which prevail over the area. Pumping has therefore become a mining operation. Of an estimated 200 million acre-feet of water which is in storage and available for pumping, some 16 million acre-feet have been withdrawn since the advent of irrigation in 1911.[15] Moreover, the annual rate of withdrawal has been following an upward trend. As a result, from 1938 to 1958 most of the irrigated portion of the South Plains experienced a decline in its water table of more than twenty feet; the most heavily irrigated portion of the area experienced a decline of over sixty feet.[16] The effect of these declines upon resource practices in the South Plains is apparent in greater pumping lifts and poorer well yields. Between 1938 and 1951, pumping lifts over the South Plains increased an average of 16 per cent and well yields decreased 18 per cent.[17] The result has been a perceptible rise in per-acre irrigation costs.

A related aspect of the declining water table is the phenomenon of drawdown. Any well that is being pumped creates a cone shaped depression in the surrounding water reservoir. This depression may extend out from the well for as much as half a mile, the distance depending upon the composition of the local water bearing formation. During the winter months, when wells are not in use, the drawdown tends to be levelled off by a lateral movement of the underground water. But during the season of heavy pumping, the drawdown gives rise to a number of problems: pumps may have to be lowered, well yields may decline, and interference with the performance of neighbors' wells may occur. Indeed, the economic limit to irrigation in the South

Plains may eventually be fixed by the drawdown rather than by any exhaustion of the water reservoir as such.[18]

Awareness of these problems came with the first surge of irrigation development in the mid-1930's. As early as 1937 some users realized that the withdrawal of ground-water was exceeding its natural recharge, and proposed the curtailment of further drilling of irrigation wells.[19] Such restriction on the development of South Plains ground-water, however, was opposed by most resource users. A bill submitted to the Texas legislature in that very year, which would have declared groundwater to be property of the state, failed of enactment.[20] It proved, though, to be the first in a long series of legislative proposals, made between 1937 and 1949, which would have licensed the drilling of irrigation wells, prorated the pumping of groundwater, modified landowners' fee simple title to groundwater, etc.[21] Most of these proposals came from outside the South Plains, reflecting the interests of cities and rural areas whose water problems were somewhat different from those of the South Plains. They were strenuously opposed by spokesmen for South Plains agricultural interests. The proposals persisted, however, as recurrent threats to maximum efficiency in the agricultural use of South Plains groundwater.

Early in 1941, a mass meeting of South Plains farmers and business men was held to discuss one of the then pending state groundwater bills. At this meeting a committee was named to investigate all future legislative developments that might concern groundwater. A resolution was also unanimously adopted opposing any legislation of state-wide scope which would regulate the use of groundwater.

Five years later, prodded by the declaration of a group of local municipal water works operators calling for state administration of groundwater, another mass meeting of farmers and landowners was held to consider the issue. A permanent water users' association was forthwith established and a resolution was unanimously adopted opposing any state groundwater regulation until more knowledge was available. During succeeding months similar water users' associations were organized in other counties of the South Plains, declaring, in the words of one, their ". . . opposition to any laws that in any way tend to regulate use of this natural resource for irrigation." [22] By early 1947, a region-wide High Plains Water Use and Conservation Association had emerged, then comprising eleven of these local associations. The new association undertook to organize regional opposition to proposed groundwater legislation by enlisting the support of other regional farm groups, sending delegates to the state capital, and publicizing its case through the local press.

Though these efforts to forestall state groundwater legislation were successful at the time, there still remained the threat of future legislation. In the words of one South Plains editor:

Legislators will soon tire of the negative attitude shown by West Texas irrigation farmers who rush to Austin to declare 'we don't want this' and 'we don't want that' at every session. Soon the legislature will ask, 'what *do* you people in West Texas want? [23]

Awareness of this problem led the High Plains Association to a revision of its strategy. With pressure mounting outside the region for some form of groundwater legislation, the association now switched to a tactic of compromise. Its full endorsement was given to an enabling bill that would authorize the establishment of groundwater conservation districts on a local option basis. Principal features of the bill were the maintenance of landowners' fee simple title to groundwater and the lack of state licensing of wells or state proration of water.[24] Fundamentally, the bill represented a strategic compromise in which South Plains resource users forestalled the threatening alternative of *state* regulation by acquiescing to a measure which might (and eventually did) subject them to *local* regulation. Enactment of the bill into law, in 1949, was construed as "a victory for the high plains water users." [25]

In these developments it is possible to glimpse the origin of the incentive to inhibit gainful resource processes. The maintenance of personal politico-economic security usually requires some compromise between various resource users and groups of resource users. In such compromise, efficiency must be exchanged for security. Resource users, if they are to avert a greater loss of gain, must acquiesce in a lesser loss of gain. Virtue can then be made of necessity and a less-gainful-but-as-likely class of resource processes will result, i.e., a class $G_i \cdot L_j$, where the elements of $G_i \cdot L_j$ are valued less than the elements of $G_j \cdot L_j$.

To further document this explanation of the origin of less gainful resource processes let us trace out the subsequent efforts of South Plains resource users to cope with the declining water table. Having succeeded in warding off state intervention in local water problems by a strategy of compromise, the High Plains Association now turned its efforts toward implementing the new enabling statute. It embarked on a campaign to establish a region-wide groundwater conservation district. Up to this point, the association had represented a coalition of individuals having rather diverse interests and opinions, all united by their common fear of state regulation of groundwater. But with this threat somewhat allayed by passage of the 1949 law, the basis of their unity had become weakened. Differences of opinion arose concerning the advisability of establishing even a locally managed groundwater conservation district. A survey, conducted just two years previously (in 1948), had asked 34 irrigation farmers and 17 community leaders this question: "Should there be any control of the use of underground water for irrigation?" Only two of the farmers answered "yes"; eight of the community leaders answered "yes." [26] In the face of such resistance to the very idea of groundwater control, the association was bound to encounter opposition to its proposed conservation district. Rival campaigns ensued, which were conducted through farmers' meetings, the press, and the radio. The range of attitudes which were expressed in these campaigns is suggested by the following expressions:

Our bill just gives us a chance to decide for ourselves how this water should be conserved. It also enables us to keep full title to it. . . . All we are trying to do is get everybody together on a conservation program of our own instead of having somebody outside tell us what to do.[27]

The irrigation farmers are now being told they must create a district to keep the federal government or some other authority from getting them, . . . How much of this is propaganda, and how much of it contains something worth considering needs careful study.[28]

The way this thing sizes up, it makes no difference what some slick-tongued agent comes out and tells you, what is on the dotted line is what counts. This thing is based on fear.[29]

The outcome, determined by elections held in September, 1951, represented a partial victory for the association. A majority of landowners in thirteen of twenty-one counties approved establishment of a High Plains Underground Water Conservation District No. 1; a majority of the landowners in eight other counties voted otherwise, thus keeping their counties out of the new district. As a result, most of the irrigated counties of the South Plains became units in a locally managed groundwater conservation district.

Inside its newly constituted jurisdiction, the water district began a vigorous educational and public relations program. The success of its endeavors is suggested by a comparative study, which was made two years after its establishment, of two counties, one belonging to the water district (Floyd county) and the other lying outside of it (Hale county).[30] This study revealed a statistically significant difference between the two counties in regard to landowners' awareness of the need for water conservation. On the basis of a 5 per cent random sample of individuals owning ten or more acres of land in the two counties, the following differences were observed: [31]

Individuals Whose Statements Indicated:	*Floyd County (within district)*	*Hale County (outside district)*
A belief that groundwater is being depleted	70	7
A belief that groundwater is not being depleted	15	59
(Chi Square = 76.52, P < .001)		
An adequate knowledge of the real source of the groundwater	32	5
An inadequate knowledge of the real source of the groundwater	53	61
(Chi Square = 18.11, P < .001)		
Total	85	66

[187]

These differences suggest something of the effectiveness of the water district's educational endeavors.

Late in 1952, confronted by further declines in ground-water levels, the water district resolved to invoke its statutory authority to require permits for drilling new irrigation wells. This decision was preceded by numerous meetings with farmers and farm groups at which the importance of well spacing as a means of averting interference through drawdown had been emphasized. On the occasion of the new rule's taking effect early in 1953, a spokesman for the water district declared as follows:

We had the choice of taking care of drilling (and) well spacing problems ourselves, or seeing other organizations move in to do it for us. It is a job that must be done if we are to continue to prosper. Every land owner can get a permit to drill a well. . . . All that we are to do is to work out well spacing so that one well will not encroach upon the rights of another land owner.[32]

In this way, the practice of well spacing has become part of the repertoire of South Plains resource processes.

Late in 1954, the water district conducted a number of exploratory meetings with farm groups with a view to discerning grass roots sentiments concerning water proration. This has long been a sensitive issue with South Plains resource users. A not uncommon reaction to the prospect of proration points up the dilemma which confronts resource users who face the threat of outside regulation; just as the water district had been regarded by many as a preferable alternative to state intervention, so voluntary proration might some day be viewed as a preferable alternative to state proration.[33]

In these developments there is manifest an incentive on the part of resource users to accede to practices that are less-gainful-than-but-as-likely-as other practices which they would prefer. Such practices may not be valued as much as the latter, but they are valued more than some others which appear as threatening prospects. In other words, practices falling in $G_i \cdot L_j$ may not be valued as much as those falling in $G_j \cdot L_j$, but they are valued more than those in $G_h \cdot L_j$.

To be sure, schismatic tendencies have persisted within the solidary front of South Plains resource users. In 1955, four years after establishment of the district, a second election was called for the purpose of admitting all or parts of three nonparticipating counties which had previously voted against the water district. Meetings were held with farm groups in the three counties and a campaign was conducted to acquaint farmers with the district's activities. The point was made that: "With more people in the district, the stronger voice we have in Austin and Washington, D. C. to combat state and federal control." [34] Division of opinion, however, was apparent in all three of the counties. Opposition leaders in one county which had found itself geographically split over the issue circulated a compromise petition which would have called for a county-limited water district—one which would be independent of the larger district. In the words of a spokesman: "If we can hold Hale County as a whole unit, we'll have a better chance to get a countywide district." [35] In the election results all three of the nonparticipating counties reaffirmed their decision to remain outside the water district.

A second schismatic tendency was one involving a member county within the water district. The occasion for the schism was an anticipated move by district officials to seek legislative amendments to the state groundwater laws. In response to this construed threat, a water users' association was organized in one county late in 1954 for the purpose of inquiring into the status and powers of the water district. Clearly motivated by fear of water proration, the new association presently became a spearhead of opposition to the water district, which at the next legislative session sponsored a bill that would clarify and extend certain powers of the district with respect to groundwater regulation. In the words of an opposition spokesman: "We do not see the right of the water district to regulate production. Proration is in the new amendment and we are against it." [36] However, the bill was enacted into law, and with this, the issue was brought to a close.

Offsetting schismatic tendencies is the ever present though now remote possibility of state intervention. A spokesman for organized labor in Texas indicated, as recently as 1957, that in his opinion groundwater reservoirs should be administered by state rather than by local agencies. Urban interests, too, concerned with their long term survival and with their ability to attract capital, have likewise advanced new proposals which bear upon the management of groundwater resources. The general prospect has been assessed by one South Plains legislator as follows:

Big city delegations are advocating all kinds of maneuvers that would force farmers to secure permits for operating their own well and that would restrict use of water within the range of the big cities. . . . Through state control, big cities hope to gain advantages that will freeze farmers out of control of their water and drive a wedge that will give the cities a say in the use of underground water.[37]

The persistence of this threatening alternative effectively inhibits the schismatic tendencies which might otherwise weaken the solidarity of South Plains resource users. Indeed, it is in many respects the *raison d'être* of that solidarity. It represents a special case of what the sociologist Sorokin has described as the "solidary effect of uniting against a common enemy." [38]

The incentive, then, to inhibit the quest for gainful resource processes, and to willingly engage in additional practices which are not gainful (or are less gainful) has its origins in the phenomenon of strategic compromise among resource users. If individuals were to heedlessly put to use all resource processes that happened to be gainful to them, or were to allow their neighbors to do so, they would bring upon themselves a long-run injury far greater than that incurred by setting bounds to their own and their neighbors' incentive for further gainful processes. But by compromising with other individuals and interests, and settling for processes that are somewhat less gainful to them, they enjoy a measure of security in that modicum of gainfulness. Hence, insofar as every resource system presupposes that its human agents work with one another, and must therefore compromise, to that extent resource practices which are less-gainful-than-but-as-likely-as the most valued ones are everywhere to be expected. The value which attaches to those practices *cannot* be compared with that which attaches to practices that are as-gainful-as-but-less-likely-than the most valued ones. Yet the conformity of fellow resource users to the one, and their abstention from the other, becomes a condition to the security of each individual resource user.

In the case of South Plains agriculture, each individual irrigation farmer has a vested interest in the conforming behavior of his fellows with reference to such practices as well spacing, avoidance of waste, etc. Any instance of closely spaced wells, wasteful drainage of fields, or disregard of regulations—however gainful it might be to some one farmer—threatens to renew the latent danger of outside pressure for state intervention in groundwater management. It is, therefore, a threat to the interests of his fellows, and may be taken as grounds for appropriate countermeasures. For instance, when one irrigation farmer in the water district's jurisdiction undertook to drill a well without a permit and in violation of spacing regulations, injunctive action was promptly taken by the district, an action which was later sustained by the courts. The prospect of such legal action ensures a high degree of likelihood to a class of less gainful resource practices, and it is essential to the maintenance of those practices over time.

With these details in mind, let us return to our theoretical problem: Why do resource users employ processes that lie within the subset $G_i \cdot L_j$ (in addition to those which lie within the subset $G_j \cdot L_j$) when the elements of $G_i \cdot L_j$ are valued less than the elements of $G_j \cdot L_j$ $(i < j)$? We may approach our problem by considering the lattice in Figure 5.

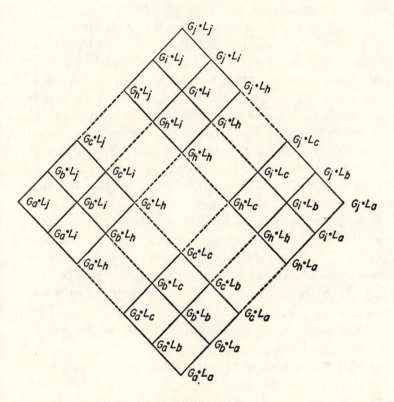

Figure 5.

In this diagram, the topmost subset $G_j \cdot L_j$ represents a type of resource process whose elements are all valued more than the elements of any of the subsets contained within it. Below this subset are two distinct chains of subsets, arranged in descending order of value. To one of these chains there corresponds the incentive to employ additional processes that are gainful to one's self, irrespective of their likelihood in others' behavior. To the other chain there corresponds the incentive to employ additional processes that are likely in the behavior of others, irrespective of their gainfulness to one's self. The first of these incentives is essentially cathectic in nature; the second is essentially cognitive.[39] Each of them prompts the resource user to add further processes to his repertoire—a fact which can be portrayed in Figure 5 as a lengthening of that portion of the relevant chain which is encompassed within the resource system. Each additional subset or type of resource process which is thus put to use (reading downward on a chain) augments the total fund of employed resource processes having the indicated magnitudes of gainfulness and likelihood; however, each such subset or type (again reading downward on a chain) has less value to the resource user than the one(s) lying above it.[40] An individual who was prompted only by the first of these two incentives would be a *homo solus;* one who was prompted only by the second of them would be an *ingénu.*

To put the matter rather elliptically, as a resource user scans the chain of subsets which is constituted by the first incentive (reading downward on the chain to the right), he perceives that every increment to his fund of gainful processes entails processes that are less and less likely in the behavior of others. As he scans the chain which is constituted by the second incentive, (reading downward to the left), he perceives that every increment to the fund of processes that are likely in the behavior of others entails processes which are less and less gainful to him. How far down these two chains, then, will the resource user reach in putting to use the elements of an adoptable set A of resource processes? Which of the subsets below $G_j \cdot L_j$ are going to have their elements incorporated as elements of a resource system X?

The answer to this question is given by the fundamental fact that in no social order can an individual resource user employ resource processes irrespective of their likelihood in others' behavior.[41] Neither can he employ resource processes irrespective of their gainfulness to himself. In the first instance, the condoning behavior of others is an essential condition to one's own personal security. In the second instance, a modicum of efficiency is an obvious condition to one's economic well-being. The reckless pursuit of gain eventually evokes repressive responses from others. Idiotic conformity impairs economic well being and eventually reduces one's very productive capacity.

What the resource user does, then, is to employ gainful resource processes up to the limit of social tolerance; he employs likely processes up to the limit of productive efficiency. To the resource processes which lie within the most valued subset $G_j \cdot L_j$ he adds both gainful and likely processes, descending down each of the two chains only so far as he can or must without incurring the penalties of undue insecurity or undue inefficiency. He performs a psychological operation of reality-testing on the subsets ranging below $G_j \cdot L_j$—an operation which manifests a certain symmetry between the contemplated actions of one human agent and the predictable reactions of other human agents.

In reality-testing, the resource user exhibits two facets to his ambivalent self. First, as an independent, free-willing "I" he presses for additional gainful-for-self processes. Second, as a dependent, conforming "me" he is pressed into additional likely-in-others processes.[42] In his first capacity he is always capable of perceiving an attractive fund of additional resource processes of the type $G_j \cdot L_h$—processes which would be fully as-gainful-for-self-as (though considerably less-likely-in-others-than) those comprising his most valued subset of processes $G_j \cdot L_j$. Illustrative of such additional processes might be the drilling of new irrigation wells at whatever sites and on whatever scale would maximize one's future net income. In his second capacity, however, the resource user is also capable of seeing the small likelihood of such processes in others' behavior. With so small a likelihood attaching to those contemplated additional processes, the resource user realistically anticipates repressive sanctions, imposed by other resource users, as a predictable consequence of his indulging in those processes. Such sanctions, he recognizes, would entail an unwanted increment of resource processes, $G_h \cdot L_j$—processes that would be as-likely-in-others-as (though considerably less-gainful-for-self-than) those comprising the most valued subset $G_j \cdot L_j$. One such threatening prospect would be the licensing, proration, and inspection of irrigation wells by a state administrative agency.

Our resource user thus finds himself in a dilemma. If he would reach down the first chain of processes (to the right) as far as $G_j \cdot L_h$, he will find himself driven down the other chain of processes (to the left) as far as $G_h \cdot L_j$. To forestall this dire prospect, he makes a strategic compromise. He foregoes his contemplated addition of resource processes of the type $G_j \cdot L_h$ and withdraws to $G_j \cdot L_i$ or even to $G_j \cdot L_j$. He settles for such processes as drilling irrigation wells only when and as they are necessary for stabilizing his present net income. Along with this, he incurs the fairly tolerable sanctions denoted by $G_i \cdot L_j$. Illustrative of such sanctions might be a program of voluntary well spacing. This subset yields an increment of processes whose gainfulness, while less than that of the subset forfeited, is greater than that to which other resource users might have driven him had he pressed his gainfulness beyond the margin of social tolerance. Moreover, it has the full measure of likelihood to which the resource user knows that his fellows can hold him accountable. The more effective these sanctions prove to be, the greater will be the resource user's withdrawal from his initial goal, $G_j \cdot L_h$. Thus, $(G_j \cdot L_i) \cdot (G_i \cdot L_j)$ represents a minimax type of resource process,[43] in which the individual, by accommodating to the behavior of his fellows and acquiescing in a lesser loss of gain, averts a greater loss of gain.[44] He finds himself conforming of his own "free will" to a subset $G_i \cdot L_j$ of resource processes whose gainfulness is less than that of the most valued subset $G_j \cdot L_j$. Inclusion in a resource system of such resource processes is, as we have already learned, the *sine qua non* of a resource complex, X'.

On the other hand, resource processes of the type $G_j \cdot L_i$ are the distinguishing feature of a resource congeries, X''. Their very existence means that the individual resource user, an "I," has been able to employ certain processes with impunity even though they are not entirely likely in others' behavior. It means that the sanctions which are represented by $G_i \cdot L_j$ have not been effective. Illustrative of such processes might be the drilling of excessively large irrigation wells. As a "me," the individual resource user may have appraised the negative reactions of others as being only token sanctions, as sanctions devoid of any real force. The exemplary behavior $G_i \cdot L_j$ of more conservation-minded resource users who, let us say, are drilling smaller wells may appear to him as only an option which he can take or leave. In this instance, there is the anomalous use, at one and the same time, by different members of a resource system, of two contrasting types of resource processes $G_j \cdot L_i$ and $G_i \cdot L_j$, processes which are as-gainful-for-self-as but less-likely-in-others-than the most valued type, and processes which are less-gainful-for-self-than but as-likely-in-others-as the most valued type. This is an anomaly which we encountered when we undertook to explain the breakdown of English open field farming (Chapter VI). There we found that the contemporaneous use, by different members of a resource system, of such contrasting types of resource processes as $G \cdot -L$ and $-G \cdot L$, indicates: (1) that the sanctions which inhere in the reactions which every resource user predicates of his fellows to his own actions are no longer effective; and (2) that some less gainful processes are being employed for no other reason than that they give token warrant to some resource users' claim that other resource users ought to do likewise. Such an anomaly, we know, is the distinguishing feature of a resource congeries, X'' as distinct from a resource complex, X'. The necessary conditions for its emergence have already been discussed, although we shall presently want to state the relationship in a more summary form.

In summary, then, the resource user who has scanned the various kinds of resource processes available to him, on a lattice of types of resource processes, will eventually put to use as many gainful processes as he dares, and as many likely processes as he must. In his capacity as an "I," he will reach down one chain of types of resource processes as far as he can without too seriously impairing his personal security. In his capacity as a "me," he will reach down the other chain of subsets as far as he must without too seriously impairing his productive efficiency. To the "I" we must ascribe the genesis of processes which are as-gainful-for-self-as, but less-likely-in-others-than, the most valued type of resource processes. To the "me" we must ascribe the genesis of processes which are less-gainful-for-self-than, but as-likely-in-others-as, the most valued type of resource processes.

We have, then, the general hypothesis that both $(G_j \cdot L_i) \cdot (G_i \cdot L_j)$ and $(G_j \cdot L_j) \cdot (G_i \cdot L_i)$ will be valued more than $(G_j \cdot L_h) \cdot (G_h \cdot L_j)$ whenever $h <, \ldots, < j$. The truth of this theorem is both tautological and synthetic. In the first instance it follows by logical inference from the particular relationship of valuation which we have postulated to hold between the elemental subsets comprising the two polynomials. In the second instance, however, it agrees with the relevant facts in an illustrative example. A correspondence thus appears to hold between: (1) the logical (algebraic) operation by which a lattice polynomial has been constructed out of the intersection of two subsets; and

(2) the psychological operation by which a resource user tests the consequences, in others' responses, of his own use of a particular type of resource process. The fact of such a correspondence gives credence to our suggestion that lattice theory may be taken as a model for an empirical theory of resource use. It encourages us, too, to formulate still further tautologies—lattice polynomials that have been constructed out of the elemental subsets $G_f \cdot L_g$ and the empirical relationships postulated to hold between those subsets—and then to predict empirical counterparts to such tautologies. Insofar as these predictions are not refuted by observation, they will constitute unfalsified hypotheses of resource use. A system of such hypotheses would constitute an unfalsified theory of resource use.

The full development of such a theory lies beyond the scope of the present study. However, one empirical finding which was reported in two of our previous chapters may be suggested as an additional postulate for the prospective theory. In Chapters VI and VII we observed that in any resource system the two dichotomous attributes $G, -G$ and $L, -L$ have their magnitudes affected by the stability or instability of the physical and cultural environment. Specifically, we found that the existence of instability (denoted by $\pi \vee \gamma \neq 0$) in the set P or the set C of physically possible and socially defined resource processes is a necessary condition for the development of a natural resource. Since the putting to use of a new natural resource is a special case of resource development, it follows that instability is a necessary condition for it too. Such use of a new natural resource, as noted in Chapter VI, is effected by a calculating opportunism which comes with the breakdown of the social sanctions that lie behind nongainful practices. By virtue of this calculating opportunism, there is an accretion to a people's complement of resource practices of some new processes which are gainful and nonlikely. The following hypothesis will generalize this observation:

$$[(G \cdot -L) < X] \supset [(\pi \vee \gamma) \neq 0].$$

According to this hypothesis, a necessary, though not a sufficient, condition for the inclusion of a new natural resource in a system of resource processes X is the existence of some instability in the physical or the cultural environment of a people. Such instability releases the incentive to employ additional gainful processes—an incentive that has hitherto been held in check by the incentive to employ those processes which are likely in, and enforceable by, other resource users in a population. Consequently, new resource processes, of the type $G \cdot -L$, can safely be put to use with little concern for the reactions of other resource users.

To incorporate this hypothesis as a postulate in a lattice of more than just four component types ($G \cdot L$, $-G \cdot L$, $G \cdot -L$, $-G \cdot -L$), we need to make one revision in our characterization of the union of the sets π and γ. Rather than considering this union to have only two possible magnitudes—empty or nonempty—let us regard it as having a range of magnitudes which form a serial. This serial, $0, \ldots, q, \ldots, r, \ldots, s$, will represent increasing *degrees* of instability in the physical or cultural environment. We may then reformulate our hypothesis to read:

$$[(G_j \cdot L_i) < X] \supset [(\pi \vee \gamma) > q],$$

where q represents an immediately prior state of the physical and cultural environment. According to this proposition, resource processes of the type $G_j \cdot L_i$ will only be added to a system of resource processes when there has been some increase in the degree of instability of a people's physical or cultural environment. This may be taken as a postulate in a general theory of resource use.

What are we to say, now, concerning the adoption and use of resource processes of the type $G_i \cdot L_j$—processes which are less-gainful-than-but-as-likely-as those which are most valued? What relationship does the use of this type of resource process bear to the stability or instability of a physical or cultural environment? Our answer to this question is going to take us full circle back to the concept of a resource complex, X', with which we were occupied in chapters III-V of this study. A resource complex, X', we will recall, is distinguished from a resource congeries, X'' by its inclusion of some processes of the type $-G \cdot L$—more specifically, of the type $G_i \cdot L_j$. In the following chapter, we shall find that a resource system of this kind is an essentially static sort of thing. Its emergence is predicated on some trend, latent if not manifest, toward stability in a people's physical and cultural environment—a trend from a higher to a lower magnitude in the union of π and γ. This postulate may be expressed in the following form:

$$[(G_i \cdot L_j) < X] \supset [(\pi \vee \gamma) \leqslant q],$$

where q represents an immediately prior state of the physical and cultural environment. In such a resource system, the type of use to which a people puts its natural resources is an indicator of the survival capacity of that people's social order. Conservation of natural resources becomes conservation of the social order. Let us take a closer look at this idea.

NOTES

* Alexander Pope, "An Essay on Man," in *The Augustans,* edited by Maynard Mack (Englewood Cliffs, N. J.: Prentice-Hall, Inc., 1950), p. 299.

1. On the methodology of defining dichotomous attributes and related concepts see: Paul F. Lazarsfeld and Allen H. Barton, "Qualitative Measurement in the Social Sciences: Classification, Typologies, and Indices," in Daniel Lerner and Harold D. Lasswell (eds.), *The Policy Sciences* (Stanford, Calif.: Stanford University Press, 1951), chap. ix; and Allen H. Barton, "The Concept of Property-Space in Social Research," in Paul F. Lazarsfeld and Morris Rosenberg (eds.), *The Language of Social Research* (Glencoe, Ill.: The Free Press, 1955), pp. 40-53.

2. The epistemological rationale for seeking "unfalsified" (rather than "verified") hypotheses in science is developed in Karl Popper, *Logik der Forschung* (Wien: J. Springer, 1935), pp. 13-16 and *passim.*

3. See: A. C. Magee, W. C. McArthur, C. A. Bonnen and W. F. Hughes, *Cost of Water for Irrigation on the High Plains* (Texas Agricultural Experiment Station Research Bulletin 745 [College Station, 1952]).

4. Riley E. Baker, "Water Development as an Important Factor in the Utilization of the High Plains of Texas," *Southwestern Social Science Quarterly,* XXXIV (1953), 21-34, citing William F. Hughes, *Cost of Pumping Water for Irrigation on the Texas High Plains* (Texas Board of Water Engineers, 1951), Appendix A, p. 18. Since 1949, however, pumping costs have been rising as a result of a decline in water levels and a consequent increase in pumping lifts. See: W. F. Hughes and A. C. Magee, *Changes in Investment and Irrigation Water Costs, Texas High Plains, 1950-54* (Texas Agricultural Experiment Station Research Bulletin 828 [College Station, 1956]).

5. Wilfrid C. Bailey, "The Status System of a Texas Panhandle Community," *Texas Journal of Science,* V (1953), 326-31.

6. *Lamesa Daily Reporter,* January 16, 1955.

7. Clyde Kluckhohn *et al.,* "Values and Value-Orientations in the Theory of Action," in Talcott Parsons and Edward A. Shils, *Toward a General Theory of Action* (Cambridge, Mass.: Harvard University Press, 1951), Part 4, p. 396.

8. This may be taken as a general datum for much of social valuation. See the statement apropos of this in Gunnar Myrdal, *An American Dilemma* (New York: Harper and Bros., 1944), Appendix I.

9. See: Nicholas Rescher and Paul Oppenheim, "Logical Analysis of Gestalt Concepts," *British Journal for the Philosophy of Science,* VI (1955), esp. 100-1.

10. It is not, however, a sufficient condition. There are elements of $G \cdot -L$ and of $-G \cdot L$ which are not put to use.

11. On lattice theory, see: Garrett Birkhoff, *Lattice Theory* ("American Mathematical Society Colloquium Publications," rev. ed., New York: American Mathematical Society, 1948), Vol. XXV. On the applications of lattice theory to social science data, see: Clyde H. Coombs, "Mathematical Models in Psychological Scaling," *Journal of the American Statistical Association,* XLVI (1951), 480-89; H. M. Johnson, "Some Neglected Principles in Aptitude Testing," *American Journal of Psychology,* XLVII (1935), 159-65; Jean Piaget, *Traité de logique* (Paris: Armand Colin, 1949); Jürgen von Kempski, "Zur Logik der Ordnungsbegriffe, besonders in den Sozialwissenschaften," *Studium Generale,* V (1952), 205-18.

12. Cf. Lazarsfeld and Barton, *op. cit.,* pp. 169-72.

13. Actually we have assumed a correspondence between a class of empirical elements and operations and a *particular kind* of lattice, viz., a Boolean algebra. Whether or not other lattices might also be taken as "models" for a theory of resource use is a question that we have not attempted to resolve. Moreover, to avoid complicating our exposition with technical intricacies that are not essential to our problem, we have employed, throughout this volume, the familiar operational symbols (V) and (·), which are customary in symbolic logic, rather than introducing the corresponding symbols which are generally used in lattice theory.

14. The hypothesis of a correspondence between mental operations and logistic operations is developed in Piaget, *op. cit.,* pp. v-vi, 10-12.

15. W. L. Broadhurst, "The Geologic and Hydrologic Aspects of the High Plains Water District," *The Cross Section* (Lubbock, Texas), I (September, 1954), 4.

16. *The Cross Section* (Lubbock, Texas), Vol. IV (May, 1958), map.

17. Hughes and Magee, *op. cit.*

18. W. L. Broadhurst, "Interference between Wells in the High Plains," *The Cross Section* (Lubbock, Texas), Vol. I (May, 1955).

19. Broadhurst, "The Geologic and Hydrologic Aspects . . ."; Ernest C. Ratliff, *A Survey, Analytical and Historical, of Irrigation in Hale County,*

Texas, Unpublished Master's thesis, Texas Technological College, 1938, p. 45.

20. Groundwater in the state of Texas is subject to common law rule, according to which percolating water is the private property of the landowner. In New Mexico, on the other hand, it is governed by a comprehensive groundwater code and by statutory controls over well drilling. See: "Summaries of the Water-Law Doctrines of the Seventeen Western States," ("President's Water Resources Policy Commission" [Washington: Government Printing Office, 1950]), Appendix B, "Water Resources Law," III, 711-77.

21. William F. Hughes, "Proposed Groundwater Conservation Measures in Texas," *Texas Journal of Science,* I (1949), 35-43.

22. Resolution quoted in *Lubbock Avalanche-Journal,* November 17, 1946.

23. *Southwestern Crop and Stock,* June, 1947.

24. Edward P. Woodruff, Jr. and James Peter Williams, Jr., "The Texas Groundwater District Act of 1949: Analysis and Criticism," *Texas Law Review,* XXX (1952), 862-75.

25. *Floyd County Hesperian,* June 16, 1949.

26. Charles Benjamin Brotherton, *The Economics of Shallow-Water Irrigation in the Texas High Plains,* Unpublished Master's thesis, Agricultural and Mechanical College of Texas, 1948, p. 76. Unfortunately no information is given us concerning the design of this sample of respondents.

27. Farmer, writing in *Plainview Evening Herald,* September 28, 1951.

28. Landowner, writing in *Plainview Evening Herald,* September 18, 1951.

29. Farmer, quoted in *Plainview Sunday Herald,* September 30, 1951.

30. Bennie Dwane Graves, *Attitudes Toward the Use and Conservation of Underground Water for Irrigation Among Farmers in Two Counties in the South Plains of Texas,* Unpublished Master's thesis, University of Texas, 1953.

31. Graves, *loc. cit.*

32. *Lubbock Evening Journal,* January 30, 1953.

33. See the *Hereford Sunday Brand,* October 31, 1954.

34. Quoted in *Ralls Banner,* December 10, 1954.

35. Quoted in *Plainview Sunday Herald,* January 9, 1955.

36. Quoted in *Lubbock Morning Avalanche,* March 10, 1955.

37. Quoted in *Hale Center American,* April 6, 1956.

38. Pitirim A. Sorokin, *Society, Culture, and Personality* (New York: Harper and Bros., 1947), p. 130. Cf. the related concept of "negative value" developed by Gideon Sjoberg and Leonard D. Cain, Jr., "Negative Values and Social Action," *Alpha Kappa Deltan,* XXIX (1959), 63-70.

39. On the theoretical derivation of these terms see: Talcott Parsons, *The Social System* (Glencoe, Ill.: The Free Press, 1951), p. 7.

40. The distinction between "valuation" (or "value") and "incentive," as the two terms have been used in this study, parallels the distinction drawn by Parsons between "evaluative orientation," on the one hand, and "cathectic orientation" and "cognitive orientation," on the other hand. See Parsons, *loc. cit.*

41. This is but a special case of a fundamental requirement of social order generally. See: Parsons, *op. cit.*, pp. 36ff.; Talcott Parsons and Edward A. Shils, "Values, Motives, and Systems of Action," *Toward a General Theory of Action* (Cambridge, Mass.: Harvard University Press, 1951), Part II, pp. 153-54, 175.

42. In this distinction between "I" and "me" we have somewhat specialized the meanings given the two terms by George H. Mead in *Mind, Self and Society* (Chicago: University of Chicago Press, 1934), pp. 173-78, 192-200.

43. We are not prepared to consider the possible affinity of this "minimax" to the minimax theorem of John von Neumann and Oskar Morgenstern, as developed in their *Theory of Games and Economic Behavior* (2nd ed., Princeton, N. J.: Princeton University Press, 1947). .

44. It will be noted that we have applied the dot symbol here to two different kinds of conjunction: first, to the intersection of magnitudes of G and L, and second, to the lattice intersection of types or subsets of $G_f \cdot L_g$.

CHAPTER IX

THE CONSERVATION
OF NATURAL RESOURCES

> . . . mere change without conserva-
> tion is a passage from nothing to
> nothing. . . . Mere conservation
> without change cannot conserve.
> For, after all, there is a flux in
> circumstance, and the freshness of
> being evaporates under mere repe-
> tition.
> ALFRED NORTH WHITEHEAD [1]

WITH SOME INDULGENCE in literary license it may be argued that resource planning is either revolutionary or reactionary. Either it is part of an effort to build a new social order, or it is part of an effort to bolster an existing social order. Programs of resource development, for example, are going to call for new social forms; programs of resource conservation, on the other hand, are going to strengthen old social forms. Hence, once we have recognized that resources have a "social" as well as a "natural" aspect, it becomes evident that any change in one will be a change in the other. Likewise, any constancy in the one will be a constancy in the other.

The argument is more than a rhetorical one. Indeed, it is the reciprocal of what we have already said concerning the necessary conditions under which different types of resource processes are put to use. At the close of the preceding chapter we suggested that new resource processes ("as-gainful-but-less-likely") can only emerge in an unstable physical or cultural environment. We also suggested that there is another type of resource process ("less-gainful-but-as-likely") which will only be found in a stable physical or cultural environment. The distinguishing feature of this second type of resource process is its *conatus,* by which the persistence of some larger whole is furthered. This larger whole is nothing other than the social order. To it we may apply the definition advanced by Spinoza: *"Conatus, quo unaquaeque res in suo esse perseverare conatur, nihil est praeter ipsius rei actualem essentiam."* "The effort by which each thing endeavors to persist in its own being is nothing else than the actual essence of the thing itself." [2] An important part of this effort by which a social order maintains itself is the set of less-gainful-but-as-likely resource processes. Such processes are inherently conservative, they conserve the social order as they conserve natural resources.

In this view of conservation, we have the conclusion of an inductive argument which must now be spelled out. Our starting point will be the proposition that conservation is a type of use. [3] Moreover, it is to be found in every viable resource system. In other words, it is a feature of a resource complex as distinct from a resource congeries. The distinguishing characteristic of resource-conserving uses, we shall assume, is the special kind of necessity which they impose on resource users. This necessity is neither physical nor logical (as is in certain respects the necessity imposed on individuals in resource development and resource use). Rather, it is a moral necessity, specifically, it is a sense of obligation. Violation of this sense of obligation contravenes values that are regarded by a people as conditions to the attainment of important ends: aesthetic, religious, familial, military, etc.[4] By virtue of the constraint thus imposed upon them, resource users acquiesce in lesser magnitudes of certain scarcity attributes; they acquiesce, that is to say, in lower consumption standards. Consequently, particular resource processes—or more precisely, the physical components of those processes—remain available to a population for a longer time than they would in the absence of that constraint.[5]

Let us then define a set N of conservation practices which will answer to the foregoing characterization. Complementary to N is the set $-N$ of nonconservation practices. Together N and $-N$ comprise a universe of resource processes. N', $-N'$ and N'', $-N''$ represent alternative differentiations of the same universe such that $N < N' < N''$ (and therefore $-N'' < -N' < -N$); i.e., we allow for three alternative cutting points between conservation and nonconservation practices. Our present interest lies in locating the set N (or, alternatively, N' or N'') within the more inclusive set A of adoptable resource processes. In our preceding chapter, we suggested that the various types of adoptable resource processes, viewed in respect to the attribute of valuation, could all be mapped on a mathematical model known as the lattice. In this realized model the valuation which resource users accord to particular types of resource processes is a two-dimensional attribute compounded out of the attributes of gainfulness and likelihood. Just where in this structure of resource processes should we expect to find resource processes of a conservational sort?

Our approach to this question has been dictated by the subjective nature of conservation practices. They are, we have said, distinguished by the sense of obligation which attaches to them. The problem, therefore, of locating conservation practices with respect to other resource processes, on the dimensions of gainfulness and likelihood, is one which will require an avowedly subjectivistic method. The procedure which we have chosen to follow involves an analysis of a sample of verbal statements in which resource users have made some profession of conservation ideals. We shall be interested in determining the sufficient conditions under which such profession of conservation ideals also signifies a sense of obligation to employ conservation practices. Previous research has shown that a belief in the value of conservation may often be combined with a very perfunctory use of conservation practices.[6] Hence, not all verbal statements on behalf of conservation can be taken as indicators of a sense of obligation on the part of resource users to employ conservation practices.[7] Only under certain conditions does the profession of conservation ideals manifest that "resistance to self" which Bergson has recognized as the quintessence of obligation.[8] And only such expressions may be taken as valid indicators of the set N of conservation practices, whose location on a lattice of resource processes we are primarily concerned with.

The verbal statements which we are about to analyze have been selected from a sample of newspapers and farm magazines published in the southern High Plains of west Texas. In compiling these statements, our first step was to specify a universe of published materials. This was defined to include all newspapers and farm magazines published in the South Plains from the beginning of 1947 through the first five months of 1955. The sample consists of: all issues of one weekly newspaper, A, which appeared in the first four or five months of odd-numbered years (state legislative months and years) from 1947 to 1955, inclusive; all issues of a regional monthly farm journal, B, which appeared in the first four or five months of odd-numbered years between 1947 and 1953; all issues of two regional irrigation periodicals, C and D, which have appeared between their founding (1952 and 1954, respectively) and May, 1955; irregularly selected issues of two daily newspapers, E and F, the dates of which coincided with legislative developments pertinent to groundwater problems between 1947 and May, 1955; and some random issues of these and other regional newspapers, G, H, I, J, K.[9]

All those articles within the sampled issues which related to groundwater resources were examined for whatever proposals, evaluations, suggestions, and criticisms might have been made or quoted. Every pertinent verbal expression was transcribed and then broken down into clauses, each clause being a unit of assertion—e.g., "We must preserve and protect our underground water in this great area" (C, Mar., 1952). Each such clause could then be categorized according to its content into one component or the other of some dichotomous attribute.[10] With a number of verbal expressions thus analyzed into clauses, and with several different attributes serving as classificatory categories for these clauses, it was possible to discern what covariations, if any, there were among the different kinds of clauses.[11] The observed covariations, in turn, served as data for a number of hypotheses about the location of conservation practices on a lattice of resource processes. Finally, these hypotheses were subjected to an empirical test and each, in the manner of Mill's method of difference, was rejected *seriatim* except one—that one remaining an unfalsified hypothesis.[12]

For the dichotomous classificatory categories recourse was had to four attributes: *idealization, obligation, likelihood,* and *comparability relative to value.*[13] Each of these attributes was dichotomized into two components: $(I, -I)$, $(O, -O)$, $(L, -L)$ and $(K, -K)$, every component being represented by a binary relation symbol, e.g., I. The "argument" of each of these components consists of any pair of resource processes $(n, -n)$, where $n \; \varepsilon \; N$ and $-n \; \varepsilon \; -N$. The eight resulting classificatory categories may be briefly characterized as follows:

1. $In, -n$, "the conservation practice n is more idealized than the non-conservation practice $-n$": connoted by expressions which assert the desirability of using groundwater resources in such a way as to assure their availability in the future. (Example: "Provide water for the next generation. Use it wisely. Find new means of conserving it." Quoted in E, Nov. 15, 1953.)

1'. $-In, -n$, "the conservation practice n is not more idealized than the non-conservation practice $-n$":[14] connoted by expressions which assert the desirability of making use of available groundwater at the present time. (Example: "But they [South Plains people] don't want to hoard water merely for the sake of hoarding it. They want to use all they can without using too much. They want to irrigate every last acre of land for which there is plenty of water, but not one acre more." E, Jan. 12, 1941.)

2. *On, —n,* "the conservation practice *n* is considered more obligatory than the non-conservation practice *—n*": connoted by expressions which assert the desirability of prohibitory or prescriptive regulations concerning individuals' use of groundwater. (Example: "It should be against the law for anyone to leave an irrigation well unattended and allow water to be wasted in this way." Quoted in E, May 3, 1953.)

2'. *—On, —n,* "the conservation practice *n* is not considered more obligatory than the non-conservation practice *—n*": connoted by expressions which assert the desirability of individual autonomy in making decisions concerning the use of groundwater. (Example: "I am not ready for anybody down at Austin to tell us how to use our water out here." Quoted in G, Jan. 10, 1941.)

3. *Ln, —n,* "the conservation practice *n* is considered more likely than the nonconservation practice *—n*": connoted by expressions which assert that there is some likelihood of impending regulations concerning the use of groundwater. (Example: "If we don't prove to the state that we are conserving, we will likely have state instead of local control." Quoted in H, Dec. 9, 1954.)

3'. *—Ln, —n,* "the conservation practice *n* is not considered more likely than the non-conservation practice

—*n": [15]* connoted by expressions which assert that there is little likelihood of impending regulations concerning the use of groundwater. (Example: "I think the threat of state control is being held over irrigation farmers without good reason." Quoted in F, Sept. 21, 1951.)

4. *Kn, —n,* "the conservation practice *n* is comparable, relative to value, with non-conservation practice —*n":* connoted by expressions which suggest that groundwater practices be judged in terms of standards of private gainfulness, thus allowing phenomenal comparability of different practices. (Example: "Using underground tile for irrigation purposes has cut the amount of water needed by one-third and the amount of labor required by two-thirds. . . . This is an experiment and a business proposition, and I can see now that it will really pay off." Quoted in E, Sept. 21, 1952.)

4'. —*Kn, —n,* "the conservation practice *n* is not comparable, relative to value, with the non-conservation practice —*n":* connoted by expressions which suggest that groundwater practices be judged in terms of standards of others' as well as private gainfulness, thus rendering some pairs of different practices phenomenally incomparable (owing to the formal impossibility of making interpersonal comparisons of gainfulness). (Example: "Conservation Irrigation to us means the use of our irrigation water as an insurance, not as a means of getting rich quickly at the expense of our water and our posterity. Conservation Irrigation should mean the prolongment of our present economy as long as possible, eliminating to a bare minimum the mining of our valuable resource for the benefit of the few of us who are using it today." D, July, 1954.)

In terms of this schema, an ideal such as conservation can be regarded as a preferential ranking of the components of the argument: "conservation," "nonconservation," or, more briefly, as a choice from the set $(In, -n, -In, -n)$. So too, the component indicated by each of the other verbal expressions quoted above can be considered as a choice from some attribute $(Fn, -n, -Fn, -n)$. Each of the foregoing pairs of characterizations defines the full range of application of a particular attribute, so that the components $In, -n$ and $-In, -n$ are complements. Given, now, the existence of a conservation ideal $In, -n$, what covariation, if any, obtains between it and the choices that are made from one or more of the other three attributes? Does a collection of verbal expressions concerning the conservation of groundwater resources exhibit any kind of semantic structure which is invariant from one verbal expression to another? Specifically, given a number of verbal expressions which connote the selection $In, -n$ rather than $-In, -n$, can one with confidence predict that those expressions will likewise denote the choice $On, -n$ rather than $-On, -n$, such that the hypothesis "*if* $In, -n$, *then* $On, -n$" is sustained? Or, rather, does such a correspondence between the rankings of the components of different attributes obtain only if certain restrictions are imposed upon $In, -n$? The problem, stated in its simplest form, is one of formulating some hypotheses about the internal composition of verbal expressions concerning groundwater conservation. It is to this problem that we may now turn.

The procedure which will be followed is that of proposing three successive hypotheses and attempting to refute each of them by adducing a falsifying instance.[16] The object in this procedure will be to attain a formulation which is falsifiable, in that it is definite and general,[17] yet one which remains unfalsified within the universe of verbal expressions defined for this study.

Consider, then, the class of all verbal expressions which connote In'', $-n''$, where $n'' \varepsilon N''$ and $-n'' \varepsilon -N''$ represent one possible differentiation between conservation practices and non-conservation practices. Subsequently, we shall have recourse to two alternative differentiations of the same universe of practices, viz., N', $-N'$ and N, $-N$. The hypothesis, then, may first be advanced that every verbal expression which asserts In'', $-n''$ will assert On'', $-n''$. By this hypothesis every idealized conservation practice would *ipso facto* be an obligatory conservation practice. To what extent, then, is the hypothesis *"if In'', $-n''$, then On'', $-n''$"* confirmed by verbal expressions found in South Plains publications? Such a hypothesis is logically equivalent to the proposition that there is no case of a verbal expression which asserts In'', $-n''$ and rejects On'', $-n''$. As such, it would appear to be falsified by the following cases of verbal expressions, each of which combines a In'', $-n''$ clause with a $-On''$, $-n''$ clause:

This new association (a county water users' association) does not oppose the conservation of water. They are for that. But they do oppose legislation and proration. (Quoted in G, Jan. 3, 1947.)

I am for water conservation, but not of the type that can be done under the present law. This law is so garbled and attached to an old surface water law that is outmoded, that nobody, even the lawyers, can give you a clear opinion of it. (Quoted in F, Sept. 21, 1951.)

We believe that there may be ways of conserving water supplies without proration. (Quoted in B, Jan., 1947.)

To be sure, verbal expressions conforming to the hypothesis are numerous, such as the following:

People of the High Plains of Texas know that the underground water table is falling. . . . This water is the life blood of the economy of the area. It is necessary, therefore, that measures be taken to bring about a balance between recharge of and withdrawal from the underground water reservoir. . . . The law under which an underground water district must be created in Texas makes possible management and conservation of underground water on the local level. (Advertisement in E, Sept. 23, 1951.)

Nevertheless, the discovery of a single instance of In'', $-n''$ conjoined with $-On''$, $-n''$ falsifies the hypothesis as a true generalization within the specified universe of verbal expressions. Apparently, there are inconsistencies between what resource users acknowledge to be good and what they acknowledge to be obligatory.

Turning, then, to a second possible covariation among the components of the attributes used in this study, it might be supposed that individual awareness of the likelihood of conservation practices, if combined with a belief in the ideal of conservation, would lead to a consideration of such practices as obligatory. That is to say, subjective certainty of the prospect of conservation practices might supposedly constrain attitudes in accordance with a psychological "reality principle." In the South Plains, we have seen, resource users have for years confronted the possibility of state legislation which would make certain conservation practices obligatory. The prospect has been variously conceived in such terms as:

. . . unless we do something about it, we will be governed by a board of water engineers at Austin. (Quoted in E, Nov. 10, 1946.)

And too, many farmers feel that state control of underground water is most imminent, therefore increasing the need for a [conservation] district of their own. It is felt that if a district is formed within the area state intervention would be out of the question. (Quoted in J, Jan. 13, 1955.)

. . . people were told that if they didn't hide behind the ground-water law . . . Texas would pass some kind of a worse law. They said even the surface laws would be revised. Well, they haven't been. (F, Sept. 30, 1951.)

Given an objectively uncertain prospect, resource users have reacted by assigning various subjective probabilities to the two alternative outcomes. There are those who consider some form of conservation to be inevitable and, hence, to be accepted or compromised by seeking the least objectionable of the proposed conservation measures, viz., a locally managed conservation program. They envision their own future resource decisions as a matter of complying with prohibitions and prescriptions imposed on them by others with respect to well drilling, pumping, and irrigating. Expressions denoting this choice may be represented by the binary relation symbol L and its "argument" (n', $-n'$), where $n' \varepsilon N'$ and $-n' \varepsilon -N'$ represent a second possible differentiation between conservation practices and non-conservation practices, N' being a proper subset of N''. Then, other resource users assert, quite to the contrary, that there is little likelihood that conservation practices will be imposed on them by others, and that resource use will continue to be of the broadly permissive type in which individual autonomy is the governing factor. Expressions of this sort may be represented thus: $-Ln'$, $-n'$.

Can, then, the prediction be sustained that every expression which asserts In'', $-n''$ and which also asserts Ln', $-n'$

will thereby assert On', $-n'$? In such a hypothesis In'', $-n''$ is restricted by its conjunction with another term—the two of which thus constitute the logical antecedent for the consequent On', $-n'$. Refutation of the hypothesis involves finding a verbal expression which asserts In'', $-n''$ and Ln', $-n'$ but which rejects On', $-n'$. Such expressions as the following seem to be of that form:

If there is a danger of confiscation of any property by either the state or the federal government, then I say let's fight with every power at our command, but never sacrifice our property rights with a flimsy campaign of appeasement. We know that the underground water resources of this area are enormous. We know that this water is our most valuable asset. We also know that it is not inexhaustible. Practically every landowner in this 21-county area treasures the water as he treasures the land itself. The proponents of this contemplated High Plains Water Control district contend that legal controls are necessary to prevent the waste of this vital resource. But the fact is, the landowner himself does conserve and protect his property, both his water and his land. The waste that the proponents say needs correcting is practically nonexistent. (Quoted in E, Sept. 26, 1951.)

We are going to have to have some kind of water conservation or we on the Plains are ruined. I grant the law is not perfect but it is something to start from and the bad points can be weeded out. Let's beat them to the draw and not let the government get control of our water, our economy's life blood. (Quoted in E, Sept. 21, 1951.)

From these instances, it would appear that not all verbal expressions which idealize conservation and which indicate awareness of its likelihood thereby acknowledge its obligatory character.

A third hypothesis may now be formulated concerning the sufficient conditions under which a verbal expression that affirms the ideal of conservation will likewise attach an obligatory character to conservation. This hypothesis postulates the existence of another clause in verbal expressions about conservation. The additional clause is one which suggests that groundwater practices be judged in terms of standards of others' *as well as* private gainfulness. An equiv-. alent clause would be one which advocated a particular *program* of resource use, insofar as the program involves ranking various groundwater practices on a scale of gainfulness for others *as well as* for the self—the locus of "others" being any collectivity residual to the self.

In the South Plains, the most effectively promoted program has been that of the High Plains Underground Water Conservation District No. 1, whose establishment we outlined in the preceding chapter. Since 1951, this public corporation has utilized, within its thirteen-county jurisdiction, both educational and regulatory methods for promoting water conserving practices. Seeking at the outset a firm base of popular support, the district concentrated initially upon a program of conservation education through publicity, lectures, and farmers' meetings. Water saving practices pertaining to the spacing of wells, the control of evaporation, and the distribution of water were contrasted with wasteful practices, and the superiority of the former, in terms of others' as well as private gain, was shown. Three years after its establishment, impelled by declining water levels throughout the South Plains and by the omnipresent threat of state intervention, the district invoked its statutory authority to require permits for drilling irrigation wells.

Any resource program, viewed as a differentiation of various resource practices on a scale of gainfulness for others as well as for self, may be regarded as a partition of the whole set of practices into two disjunct subsets: the specifically prescribed and the nonprescribed.[18] Verbal expressions which advocate such a program may invoke standards of private gainfulness or standards of others' gainfulness. In the former case, the partition of resource practices into the prescribed and the nonprescribed subsets can be rationalized in terms of the relative magnitudes of some one attribute (or commensurable attributes), such as profitability, capital gain, or crop yield. Here there is a subjective or phenomenal comparability, from the resource user's point of view, of every pair of alternative resource practices, irrespective of their belonging to the prescribed or the nonprescribed subsets; any two practices can be ranked to form a complete ordering with respect to value.

On the other hand, verbal expressions which rationalize a resource program in terms of others' as well as private gainfulness perforce render some pairs of prescribed and nonprescribed practices incomparable with respect to value. There is no way of comparing the subjective gainfulness of different individuals, or of groups versus individuals. The partition, therefore, must find its verbal justification in some incommensurable properties—e.g., sentiment *as well as* profitability, organizational commitment *as well as* crop yield, etc. A justification of this kind, by requiring choice according to different criteria, allows no ranking of practices on a single ordinal scale of valuation but, like the classical distinction between the sacred and the profane, creates a division ". . . into two classes which embrace all that exists, but which radically exclude each other." [19]

This relation of incomparability, which finds no systematic formulation in theories of social choice,[20] may be represented by the binary relation symbol $-K$ and its "argument" $(n, -n)$ to be read: "The conservation practice n is not comparable, relative to value, with the nonconservation practice $-n$." Here $n \, \varepsilon \, N$ and $-n \, \varepsilon \, -N$ represent a third possible differentiation between conservation practices and nonconservation practices, and $N < N' < N''$.

In terms of the universe of published materials defined for this study the hypothesis may be advanced that any verbal expression which, on grounds of others' welfare, suggests a commitment of resource users to a definite program of resource management, and which asserts the desirability and the likelihood of some form of conservation, will acknowledge the obligatoriness of conservation. The hypothesis affirms that every verbal expression which asserts the conjunction $(In'', -n'') \cdot (Ln', -n') \cdot (-Kn, -n)$ will assert $On, -n$. Illustrative of the hypothesis is this expression:

The declining level of underground water on the high plains brings us face to face with the fact that something must be done to conserve the water if this country is to continue to be the highly productive area it has been. The High Plains Underground Water Conservation Association is trying to take the lead in that matter. We are glad that the plains area of Floyd County is a member of that Association and we are sorry that some parts of the plains, notably Hale County, has so far refused to come into it. Of course the success of the organization's efforts will be determined to some extent on cooperation from all the shallowater area. We don't understand why these areas refuse to join the organization. Perhaps they have a good and sufficient reason that hasn't been explained to us. Or perhaps it is a selfish attitude that says, "We will pump water out of the ground as fast and as much as we please and let the future generations take care of themselves." That sort of attitude is one that is most likely to bring on state control of underground water and then those boys who get so upset over the prospect of local control will really have something to get upset about. (G, quoted in H, Jan. 13, 1955.)

Refutation of the hypothesis would entail finding a verbal expression in which the antecedent conjunction of terms was asserted but the consequent, $On, -n$, was rejected. No such expressions were yielded by the sample of published materials selected for this study.

Of course, failure to falsify the hypothesis in no sense amounts to its confirmation; however, its credibility within the defined universe of published materials becomes somewhat greater. Similarly, failure to falsify the hypothesis is no warrant for inferring a causal connection between the antecedent clauses and the consequent clause of a verbal expression. The method of difference permits only an elimination of supposed but fallacious causes, not the demonstration of actual causal relationship. Hence, the hypothesis can be regarded only as having more approximately identified a sufficient (though not necessary and sufficient) condition for $On, -n$ than did the two falsified hypotheses. Finally, the empirical generality of the hypothesis can be assessed only through comparative research, in which a more inclusive universe of verbal expressions has been defined.

With these reservations in mind, it may be profitable to press the inquiry one step further. By means of logical rules of inference the hypothesis

(1) $(In'', -n'') \cdot (Ln', -n') \cdot (-Kn, -n) \supset (On, -n)$

can be transformed into its contrapositive

(2) $(-On, -n) \supset (-In'', -n'') \lor (-Ln', -n') \lor (Kn, -n),$

both understood as universally quantified statements.[21] By reference to the four attributes used in this study the transformed hypothesis may be read: Any verbal expression which asserts the desirability of individual autonomy in the use of groundwater will assert the desirability of making use of available groundwater at the present time, and/or will assert that there is little likelihood of impending regulations concerning groundwater, and/or will suggest that groundwater practices be judged in terms of standards of private gainfulness. Refutation of this hypothesis, of course, would constitute refutation of its equivalent (equation 1), though this was not afforded by any of the verbal expressions within the study sample.

Equation 2, though logically equivalent to equation 1, orients our attention in a somewhat different direction. By reversing antecedent and consequent clauses, it identifies a necessary condition of $-On, -n$. That is to say, it identifies a necessary condition for the lack of a sense of obligation concerning the use of natural resources. Equation 1, on the other hand, identifies a sufficient condition for a sense of obligation concerning the use of natural resources. Both types of statements are represented in the verbal expressions which have been sampled from South Plains newspapers and farm magazines.

We have said, now, that the attribute $(On, -n, -On, -n)$ is the *differentia specifica* of conservation versus nonconservation practices. In the first component of this attribute there is depicted a sense of obligation with respect to conservation practices; in the second and complementary component there is depicted a sense of individual autonomy with respect to conservation practices. Equations 1 and 2 give us the respective conditions for these two components. What bearing, now, do these findings have upon the problem of locating the set N of conservation practices on a lattice of resource processes, where the constituent dimensions are given by the attributes of gainfulness and likelihood? What correspondence may there be between various types of resource processes, viewed in respect to their attributes of gainfulness and likelihood, and a number of verbal expressions concerning resource processes, classified in terms of the attributes of idealization, likelihood, and comparability relative to value? With regard to this problem it will be instructive to take another look at equations 1 and 2.

We may begin with the first of them. In the discussion which follows we shall revert to our previous four-element lattice which is comprised of the subsets or types $G \cdot L$, $G \cdot -L$, $-G \cdot L$ and $-G \cdot -L$. This decision is imposed on us by the gross nature of our data (the verbal expressions), the use of which allows us to do no more than dichotomize each of the four attributes of idealization, obligation, likelihood, and comparability relative to value. In the foregoing empirical analysis, for example, any particular n could have only the relation L or the relation $-L$ to any particular $-n$; serialization of the relation of likelihood, as well as of the other three attributes, was not possible with the data at hand. Given, then, the partial ordering of $G \cdot L$, $G \cdot -L$, $-G \cdot L$, and $-G \cdot -L$ with respect to value, as depicted in Figure 6, three hypotheses may be proposed, consistent with equation 1, concerning the location of the set N of conservation practices on a lattice of resource processes:

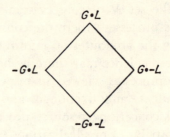

Figure 6.

1. From In'', $-n''$ we hypothesize that the elements n'' of the set N'' of conservation practices can be in any one or all of the four types comprising a four-element lattice of types of resource processes.

2. From Ln', $-n'$ we hypothesize that all of the elements n' of the set N' are in either or both of the types $-G \cdot L$ and $G \cdot L$.

3. From $-Kn$, $-n$ we hypothesize that all of the elements n of N are in either or both of the types $-G \cdot L$ and $G \cdot -L$.[22]

The combination of these three conditions makes N a subset of $-G \cdot L$. In other words, conservation practices are to be numbered among the nongainful but likely resource practices of a population. This is the conclusion to which our inductive argument, tentative though it be, would seem to lead us. It is a conclusion, moreover, which is reinforced by certain plausibility considerations that may be advanced regarding the "then" constituent of equation 1, viz., *On, —n.* These considerations stem from a closer look at two of the attributes in the "if" constituent of the equation, viz., *Ln', —n'* and *—Kn, —n.*

Likelihood, we have said, is a subjective quality which one resource user attributes to the behavior of other resource users. What, now, is the subjective counterpart, *in these other resource users,* of a given resource user's attribution of likelihood to their behavior? Surprisingly enough, it is the attribute of gainfulness. That is to say, what appears to one individual as likely in another's behavior appears to that other individual as gainful for himself. Otherwise he would not engage in it and it would not appear to others as likely in his behavior. This interpretation calls for some elaboration.

Let us proceed to make a series of substitutions in the four types which constitute the subsets of Figure 6:

For:		*Substitute:*
$G \cdot L$	↔	gainful for self & gainful for others
$G \cdot -L$	↔	gainful for self & nongainful for others
$-G \cdot L$	↔	nongainful for self & gainful for others
$-G \cdot -L$	↔	nongainful for self & nongainful for others

These substitutions may then be entered on a four-element lattice, as in Figure 7:

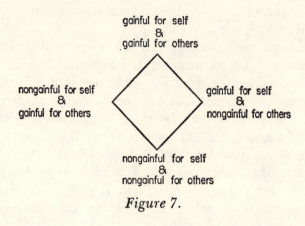

Figure 7.

In this rendition of our schema we gain a new insight into the nature of conservation practices. Their obligatory character is, we have already seen, conditional upon their likelihood in others' behavior and upon their incomparability (relative to value) with nonconservation practices, as well, of course, as upon their idealization. That is to say, a practice will be considered obligatory if it is perceived as being *likely in others' behavior* and as being incomparable to some other practice (relative to value). In our new rendition, this hypothesis may be expressed as follows: A practice will be considered obligatory if it is perceived as being *gainful for others* and as being incomparable to some other practice (relative to value). What, now, is the present significance of the condition "incomparable . . . relative to value," when value is measured on the two newly characterized dimensions of gainfulness for self and gainfulness for others? The significance of this condition lies precisely in the fact that an individual has taken over, *as his own,* the standards of gainfulness for others as well as the standards of gainfulness for himself. The private gainfulness of others has become the moral gainfulness of the self. The individual, in short, has acquired a conscience.[23] He now judges various pairs of resource practices in terms of two heterogeneous standards. One of them is private and egoistic; the other is moral and altruistic. Each represents an incentive for putting to use corresponding types of resource processes. The one gives warrant to the use of processes which are gainful-for-self-and-nongainful-for-others; the other gives warrant to the use of practices which are nongainful-for-self-and-gainful-for-others. Both represent components of the composite dimension of valuation. In conservation behavior, as in obligatory behavior generally, the first of these incentives is inhibited (though with some ambivalence) and only the latter achieves manifest expression. The ultimate source of the inhibition, of course, is supplied by the quality of likelihood in others' behavior. Conservation practices, therefore, fall entirely within the one type, nongainful-for-self-and-gainful-for-others, on Figure 7. This, of course, is but another way of expressing our earlier formulation of the same point, viz., that the set N of conservation practices is a proper subset of the set $-G \cdot L$ of resource processes.

In a roundabout way we have thus arrived at a conception of conservation which agrees with much of classical thinking about obligatory behavior generally. There is, first of all, an "antagonism to some inclination," [24] a "resistance to self," [25] in all obligation. This resisted inclination is nothing other than the egoistic incentive; in the special case of resource behavior, it is the incentive to employ processes that are privately gainful in respect to economic efficiency. Second, in obligation generally, "a social ego is superadded, in each of us, to the individual self." [26] This superadded ego yields the altruistic incentive; in resource behavior, it is the incentive to employ processes that are gainful to others in respect to economic efficiency, i.e., to comply with what is likely in others' behavior. Thus, while obligation resides in the relationship of the self to others,[27] it differs from arbitrary constraint of the self in the fact that, as Bergson put it, "Obligation, which we look upon as a bond between men, first binds us to ourselves." [28] Its locus, in other words, is in the individual conscience. This is the important point. It means that obligation resides *within* as well as *without* the individual; it has interiority as well as exteriority.

In this respect, the findings of the present chapter put an altogether new light on our previous analysis of the incentive to employ nongainful practices—of which resource-conserving uses, and obligatory behavior generally, represent special cases. It now appears that resource practices which are privately nongainful, such as conservation behavior, involve a great deal more than mere expedience in an individual's relationships with his fellows. An individual's acknowledgment that a particular practice is obligatory for him is apparently not ensured when he professes to idealize that practice and perceives it as being likely in the behavior of his fellows. In'', $-n''$ and Ln', $-n'$ do not invariably imply On', $-n'$. There is another quality which has to be attributed by that resource user to the practice in question before he will acknowledge that it is obligatory for him to observe it. This additional quality, $-Kn$, $-n$, is an ambivalent subjection of the practice to standards of others' as well as private gainfulness, the former having now become constitutive of the individual's conscience and yielding a moral gainfulness to him. This, we may recall, is a conclusion to which we were led, by a different route, as early as Chapter VI.

The attribute of likelihood, it appears, can only endow a resource practice with the aspect of exteriority for resource users. At times it may render conformity the expedient course of conduct. But it is the ambivalent commitment of resource users to standards of others' as well as private gainfulness which endows a practice with the aspect of interiority for resource users. This ambivalent commitment is reflected in the attribute of incomparability (relative to value) between particular pairs of resource processes. It is this attribute $(-Kn, -n)$ which converts what is good $(In'', -n'')$ and what is sure $(Ln', -n')$ into what is right and obligatory, yielding thus the triadic composition of obligatory resource practices as "the good, the sure and the right." It accomplishes this end by equipping the resource user with two distinct and incommensurable standards of gainfulness: the private, or egoistic, and the moral, or altruistic.[29] The first, by itself, could never yield a viable resource system. In the words of Durkheim, "There is nothing less constant than interest. Today it unites me to you; tomorrow it will make me your enemy."[30] A viable resource system, like a viable social order, must rest upon a fund of moral sentiments which provide standards of gainfulness that are quite heterogeneous to the private, egoistic standards. "Altruism," notes Durkheim, "is not . . .

a sort of agreeable ornament to social life, but it will forever be its fundamental basis." [31] This would appear to be the case with every viable resource system.

Equation 2, as the contrapositive of equation 1, points up these conclusions in another way, by specifying some of the necessary (though not sufficient) conditions for the disavowal, by resource users, of a sense of obligation concerning conservation practices. Specifically, from a resource user's assertion that individual autonomy should be the desideratum in resource decision making we can conclude that one (or a combination) of three circumstances obtains:

Either: 1. $-In''$, $-n''$, in which case the elements $-n''$ of the set $-N''$ of nonconservation practices are excluded from none of the four types on a four-element lattice of types of resource processes.

And/or: 2. $-Ln'$, $-n'$, in which case the elements $-n'$ of the set $-N'$ are excluded only from the types $G \cdot -L$ and $-G \cdot -L$.

And/or: 3. Kn, $-n$, in which case the elements $-n$ of the set $-N$ are excluded from the types $G \cdot -L$ and $-G \cdot L$.

Under none of these conditions are elements $-n$ of $-N$ excluded from the subset $G \cdot L$. In other words, under any one of these conditions nonconservation practices may be numbered among the gainful and likely practices of a population. And under any of these conditions resource users may feel no moral compunctions whatever about the kinds of resource processes which they employ. Their disavowal of an obligatory character to conservation practices means that they do not idealize such practices, or that they do not perceive such practices as being likely in others' behavior, or that they consider such practices to be fully comparable to nonconservation practices (relative to value). The first two conditions are clear enough. The third one, however, calls for some explanation.

We have said that conservation consists of the maintenance of social capital. More specifically, it involves prolonging into the future the availability of certain physical resource processes by the device of reducing a population's present consumption standards. As such, conservation represents diseconomic behavior. It is a form of investment in which the marginal revenues that a resource will yield fall short of its marginal costs, over whatever periods of time resource users are able to realistically plan. Conservation achieves this end, quite literally, by obstructing the individual's capacity to completely order alternative resource processes on a single scale of valuation. In place of such a unidimensional ordering of resource processes it endows the individual with two distinct and heterogeneous standards for judging value—one, moral and altruistic, the other, private and egoistic. It thereby confounds him and renders him a less rational—indeed, a non-rational—decision maker. The resulting incomparability between pairs of conserving and nonconserving resource processes we have symbolized as $-Kn, -n$.

In nonconservation behavior, on the other hand, there may be what Ciriacy-Wantrup has called a "calculative, antitraditional, and materialistic (if not outright pecuniary) approach" to resource decisions.[32] The resource user in this case becomes the rational *homo oeconomicus*, devoid of conscience, capable of completely ordering a set of available resource processes with respect to value (his standard being that of private gainfulness) and then putting to use only those which afford him a least cost combination of productive factors. Such a resource user thus selects for use only those resource processes which fall within the upper range of a scale of private gainfulness. Indeed, this is his only scale of valuation. The resulting comparability of every pair of resource processes, nonconserving as well as conserving ones, we have symbolized as Kn, $-n$. It represents one of the possible conditions of nonconserving resource uses and of nonobligatory behavior generally.

There are, of course, only two types of resource processes that are relevant to a resource system that is characterized by the attribute Kn, $-n$, viz., $G \cdot L$ and $-G \cdot -L$, or, in our newer rendition: (1) processes which are gainful-for-self-and-gainful-for-others, and (2) processes which are nongainful-for-self-and-nongainful-for-others. Only these two types answer to the requirement that every pair of resource processes be comparable, relative to value. A resource system constituted of such resource processes will be a completely ordered system, with private gainfulness being the ordering criterion. The question now arises: is such a system a viable one? Clearly enough a resource system of this kind is going to be one which sloughs off processes that lie in the subset $-G \cdot -L$, since these are processes that have no value for resource users by any criterion. In the limiting case, therefore, a system which is characterized by the attribute Kn, $-n$ will have all of its elements situated in the subset $G \cdot L$, comprising processes that are gainful-for-self-and-gainful-for-others. This, of course, is the subset in which we should expect to find the resource processes that characterize a freely competitive market economy—one in which a price system, operating as an "invisible hand," effects a perfect coincidence between the *salus individualis* and the *salus rei publicae*. Marginalist economic theory offers a systematic account of such a coincidence.

Our own inquiries, of course, have established the fact that not all of the resource practices of a people are, or could be, contained within this subset of processes. The reason, we know, lies in the necessity for co-operation among interdependent resource users and the corollary necessity for predictability in their personal relationships. A competitive market economy, like any other system characterized by the attribute $Kn, -n,$ is one that "can only give rise to transient relations and passing associations." [33] No viable resource system, and no viable social order, can be built upon self-interest alone. As an ideal type, to be sure, the notion of a coincidence between self-interest and the interest of others may be of help in assessing the significance of empirical departures from it. But as a predictive theory of resource behavior, it is manifestly inadequate. As a policy norm, it can be grossly misleading. Indeed, in its terms there would be no rationale whatever for conservation practices. Such practices, by our definition, are never privately gainful. [34] They are predicated, instead, on a sense of obligation, on an ambivalent attitude with respect to gainful and nongainful processes. Conservation practices partake of the same attitude which sustains every social order: the attitude of willing conformity, with all its attending limitations upon self-interested behavior. One does not find this attitude in resource practices that are gainful-for-self-and-gainful-for-others. One finds it only in practices that are nongainful-for-self-and-gainful-for-others. Here then is where we must look for the *conatus* by which a social order maintains itself.

By now it will be apparent that in this characterization of conservation we have perforce revealed the unique feature of a resource complex X', as distinct from a resource congeries X''. Common to both kinds is, of course, the optimal subset $G \cdot L$. But there the resemblance ends. In a resource complex there are no processes of the type $G \cdot -L$, and the very incentive to employ such processes has been psychologically repressed. Meanwhile the contrary incentive to employ processes of the type $-G \cdot L$ has found its realization in actual behavior. Productive efficiency has yielded to prudence and conscience, and the resource user, like Hicks's monopolist, has achieved that most enviable of goals, a quiet life.

Such a resource system, however, can develop only where there is some degree of stability in a people's physical and cultural environment. Stability in these parameters reduces the scope of the "big chance," wherein the wayward individual can afford to break with the expectations of his fellow resource users and pursue gainful and nonlikely processes. Stability in these parameters renders an individual's future prospects more contingent upon his present relationships with other resource users; any violation of others' expectations comes to have an irreversibility in its impact upon personal relationships which is harder to live down than would be the case where objective opportunities for gain were in flux. Hence in a stable physical and cultural environment, it is prudent for every resource user to set bounds to his pursuit of privately gainful processes, to exchange efficiency for security, and to discover the truth in Plato's observation that virtue is but long range self interest. Then, for the individual, what was prudent becomes right; what was likely becomes obligatory. The individual becomes his own tyrant, repressing (with some ambivalence) his incentive to pursue gainful but nonlikely processes, and willingly conforming to the practices of his fellow resource users.

The dynamics by which these developments take place are present in every social order. The greater the degree of stability in a physical and cultural environment the more nearly those dynamics will be able to run their full course to the point of yielding a resource complex. Even in an unstable environment, however, they are present in latent or virtual form. This can be seen in the southern High Plains of North America. During all of its recorded history, the South Plains has known a volatile succession of resource congeries, each of them being a response to some alteration in the physical or cultural environment. Yet even in this region, the latent dynamics by which resource processes get "moralized," as it were, can be readily identified. As irrigation know-how, for instance, has become more firmly established, as knowledge of the realities of groundwater phenomena has become more general, and as the consequences of proper and improper irrigation have become clearer, an idealization of certain kinds of resource processes has emerged. In other words, with a trend toward stabilization in the cultural environment of South Plains resource users, there has evolved some preference for practices that are deemed "good." This very stabilization has also occasioned concern among other resource users (mainly outside the region), who have resorted to legislative maneuvers that have rendered some of the "good" practices "sure" as well. Finally, with stabilization of this irrigation culture there has come, in the minds of some resource users, a dedication, on behalf of others, to the cause of "good" and "sure" practices—an acknowledgment that others' advantage as well as their own must figure in resource behavior—an acceptance, in short, of certain resource practices as being morally "right." Out of this triad of attitudes has developed a sense of obligation on the part of some resource users toward certain resource practices. It is by just this kind of development that nongainful and likely practices insinuate themselves into people's thinking and, abetted by a stable environment, enter into behavior as elements of a resource complex. Such practices then become supports of the social order, contributing to its maintenance and resisting its change.

NOTES

1. Alfred North Whitehead, *Science and the Modern World* (New York: Macmillan Co., 1946), p. 250.

2. Quoted in E. S. Russell (trans.), *The Directiveness of Organic Activities* (Cambridge: Cambridge University Press, 1946), p. 191.

3. Cf. S. V. Ciriacy-Wantrup, *Resource Conservation* (Berkeley and Los Angeles: University of California Press, 1952), p. 51; Anthony Scott, *Natural Resources: the Economics of Conservation* (Toronto: University of Toronto Press, 1955), pp. 17-19; Erich W. Zimmermann, *World Resources and Industries* (rev. ed.; New York: Harper and Bros., 1951), pp. 806-7.

4. I have analyzed this phenomenon as a general datum for land use theory in my *Land Use in Central Boston* (Cambridge, Mass.: Harvard University Press, 1947), chaps. iii-v.

5. This characterization of conservation is essentially a social-psychological one, although it appears to be compatible with the economic defi-

nition of conservation proposed by Ciriacy-Wantrup (*op. cit.*, pp. 51-52) and with Zimmermann's distinction between "conservation" and "conservancy" (*op. cit.*, pp. 806-7).

6. E.g., Edward O. Moe, *New York Farmers' Opinions on Agricultural Policies and Programs* (Cornell Extension Bulletin 864 [Ithaca, N. Y., 1952]), pp. 41ff.; John C. Frey, *Some Obstacles to Soil Erosion Control in Western Iowa* (Iowa Agricultural Experiment Station Research Bulletin 391 [Ames, Oct., 1952]), pp. 951, 958, 981; C. R. Hoglund, *Soil Conservation in Michigan—Progress and Problems* (Michigan Agricultural Experiment Station Special Bulletin 394 [East Lansing, 1955]), pp. 11-13.

7. For a systematic treatment of consistency and inconsistency in personality and culture, see: Pitirim A. Sorokin, *Society, Culture, and Personality* (New York: Harper and Bros., 1947), pp. 325-32, 342-58; Robert K. Merton, *Social Theory and Social Structure* (Glencoe, Ill.: The Free Press, 1949), pp. 133-47.

8. Henri Bergson, *The Two Sources of Morality and Religion,* trans. by A. Ashley Audra and Cloudesely Brereton (New York: Henry Holt and Co., Inc., 1935), p. 12.

9. Names of the periodicals are: A, *Floyd County Hesperian;* B, *Southwestern Crop and Stock* (Lubbock, Tex.); C, *Texas Hi-Plains Irrigation Journal* (Lubbock, Tex.); D, *The Cross Section* (Lubbock, Tex.); E, *Lubbock Morning Avalanche, Lubbock Evening Journal;* F, *Plainview Evening Herald;* G, *Lockney Beacon;* H, *Tulia Herald;* I, *Muleshoe Journal;* J, *Lamesa Daily Reporter;* K, *Hale Center American.*

10. Which would sometimes be contingent on that of adjacent clauses.

11. The covariations in question were to have an all-or-none rather than a correlational character. Accordingly, the categorization of clauses amounted to a non-frequency type of content analysis, in which the quantities (number of clauses) were simply 1 or 0. Berelson has proposed the designation "content assessment" for this type of analysis. (Bernard Berelson, *Content Analysis in Communication Research* [Glencoe, Ill.: The Free Press, 1952], pp. 119-21). In the absence of any canons of sample design for non-frequency analysis, the foregoing descriptive account of the sample must suffice.

12. On the method of difference, see Morris R. Cohen and Ernest Nagel, *An Introduction to Logic and Scientific Method* (New York: Harcourt, Brace and Co., 1934), pp. 256-59. An epistemological rationale for seeking "unfalsified" rather than "verified" hypotheses in science is developed in Karl Popper, *Logik der Forschung* (Wien: J. Springer, 1935), pp. 13-16.

13. Idealization will be understood as a type of valuation in which the individual resource user is either noncommittal or ignorant of the precise standard which he is using in evaluating different resource processes. It amounts, therefore, to ranking processes on some one dimension which remains unformulated by the human agent.

14. I.e., is equally idealized with, or is less idealized than.

15. I.e., is considered as likely as or less likely than.

16. These three hypotheses do not exhaust the logically possible hypotheses that might be built out of the four indicated attributes and their respective components. Altogether some twenty-six such hypotheses might be formed by varying the number and the sign of the attributes which can be postulated as logically antecedent to the consequent $On, -n$. The three hypotheses which have been selected for our present analysis were dictated by nothing more than plausibility considerations. Hence the significance of our "final" unfalsified hypothesis must be appropriately qualified.

17. Cf. Popper, *op. cit.*, pp. 46, 67, 75. On the rationale for deviant case analysis, see Popper, pp. 13-16; and Patricia L. Kendall and Katherine M. Wolf, "The Two Purposes of Deviant Case Analysis," in Paul F. Lazarsfeld and Morris Rosenberg (eds.), *The Language of Social Research* (Glencoe, Ill.: The Free Press, 1955), pp. 167-70.

18. "Nonprescribed" in the sense of unspecified, hence inclusive of allowable or condoned, as well as prohibited practices.

19. Emile Durkheim, *The Elementary Forms of the Religious Life* (Glencoe, Ill.: The Free Press, 1947), p. 40.

20. Cf. the postulate of Kenneth J. Arrow that "any two alternatives are comparable" (*Social Choice and Individual Values* [New York: John Wiley and Sons, Inc., 1951], p. 13), and the assumption by John von Neumann and Oskar Morgenstern of the completeness of a system of preferences (*Theory of Games and Economic Behavior* [2nd ed.; Princeton: Princeton University Press, 1947], p. 26).

21. A full rendition of equation 1 would be as follows:

$$(t, E, S, n'', n', n, I, L, K, O) \ [\{Et \cdot St \ (In'', -n'')\} \cdot \{Et \cdot St \ (Ln', -n')\} \cdot \\ \cdot \ \{Et \cdot St \ (-Kn, -n)\} \supset \{Et \cdot St \ (On, -n)\}],$$

where t denotes any thing, E denotes the property of being a verbal expression, S denotes the property of asserting or suggesting, and n, I, L, K, O have the previously defined meanings. In this equation, the relational attributes I, L, and O are all asymmetrical, whereas $-K$ is symmetrical. There is an interesting correspondence between the notation which we have here employed and that used by Karl Menger, in his *Moral, Wille und Weltgestaltung* (Wien: J. Springer, 1934), pp. 69-80, which may be summarized as follows:

Our notation	Menger's notation
$n, -n$	V
O	N
$On, -n$	$N(V)$
$In, -n$	$n(V)$
$- - -$	M_t

In Menger's terms we have been looking for the sufficient conditions such that, for all M_i of which n_{M_i} (V) is true, N_{M_i} (V) is likewise true. An important formalization of obligatory behavior is to be found in: Alan Ross Anderson and Omar Khayyam Moore, "The Formal Analysis of Normative Concepts," *American Sociological Review*, XXII (1957), 9-17.

22. I.e., there is nothing in In'', $-n''$ that would exclude n'' ϵ N'' from any of the four types. Even the least valued type, $-G$ • $-L$, may have some of its elements more idealized than some other elements. Ln', $-n'$, on the other hand, by definition limits n' ϵ N' to the two types which have an L component. $-Kn$, $-n$, again by definition, limits n ϵ N to the two types which are not comparable $(-K)$ in terms of value.

23. The concept of moral gainfulness, it should be noted, does no violence to our initial definition of gainfulness as the upper range of a psychological magnitude which corresponds to a high degree of productive efficiency. In the case of moral gainfulness the beneficiaries of productive efficiency are others rather than the self, yet the self, by virtue of its antecedent conditioning, actually "wishes" this outcome.

24. Thomas Hill Green, *Lectures on the Principles of Political Obligation* reprinted from his *Philosophical Works* (London: Longmans, Green and Co., Ltd., 1941), II, 125.

25. Bergson, *op. cit.*, p. 12.

26. *Ibid.*, p. 7.

27. L. T. Hobhouse, *Morals in Evolution* (3d. ed.; London: Chapman and Hall, 1915), chaps. vii-viii.

28. Bergson, *op. cit.*, p. 7.

29. Arrow, *op. cit.*, pp. 82-83.

30. Emil Durkheim, *The Division of Labor in Society* (Glencoe, Ill.: The Free Press, 1933), pp. 203-4; See too, Talcott Parsons, *The Structure of Social Action* (New York: McGraw-Hill Book Co., 1937), pp. 402-4.

31. Durkheim, *op. cit.*, p. 228. For an empirical and theoretical analysis of the conditions and characteristics of altruism as a social datum, see Pitirim A. Sorokin, *Explorations in Altruistic Love and Behavior* (Boston: Beacon Press, 1950), chap. i.

32. Ciriacy-Wantrup, *op. cit.*, p. 90.

33. Durkheim, *op. cit.*, p. 204.

34. Resource-prolonging activities which *are* privately gainful should be given their own distinguishing appellation. Zimmermann has proposed the term "conservancy" for this class of practices. In his words, "*Conservation* is any act reducing the rate of consumption or exhaustion for the avowed purpose of benefiting posterity. . . . *Conservancy* means reduction in the rate of exhaustion of a natural resource which is not sought for its own sake but is incidental to the exercise of economy." *Op. cit.*, p. 807. His emphases.

CHAPTER X

CONSENT AS A CONDITION
OF RESOURCE PLANNING

> The strongest is never strong
> enough to be always the master,
> unless he transforms strength into
> right, and obedience into duty.
> JEAN JACQUES ROUSSEAU

COMMON SENSE can have a blighting effect upon planning. The reason for this paradox lies in the *ad hoc*
character of common sense statements. Their truths are
contingent; they are unsystematic; and they are unrelated
to other truths in any specified way. The resource planner
or policy maker who would eschew theory for common
sense is likely to find himself relying on contradictory
precepts to guide him in his decision making.

In no area of planning is this more true than in the area
of natural resources. "Of course we should develop idle

resources for use." "Of course we should conserve resources for posterity." In these two "self evident" assertions there is likely to be, for the unwary at least, a real contradiction. No amount of factual information can dispel the confusion that may arise out of relying upon discrete statements such as these. Nothing less than a systematic theory, one which remains unfalsified by experience, can serve as an adequate instrument for rational decision making in resource development and conservation.

It has been our purpose in this study to establish some of the propositions that might enter into such a theory. In effect, what we have done is to specify one of the conditions of effective resource planning, viz., consent. We have done this through demonstrating that certain constellations of attitudes represent conditions for resource users' engaging in particular types of resource processes. The planner who would realize one or another of those types of resource processes, then, is well advised to look to the attitudes which his resource users, as "plannees," may have.

It is true, of course, that consent is not a necessary condition of successful planning. Draconian measures have, in many social orders, attained objectives that could never have been attained on the basis of popular consent. It is true, too, that there is a certain redundancy in plans that do no more than reiterate objectives which resource users would pursue anyway. If plans are to be analytically independent of their subjects' preferences, and are nevertheless to be realized—if plans are to "make a difference"—their formal properties and their formal conditions must be clearly understood. Let us address ourselves to this problem.

Consent as a Condition of Resource Planning

A plan can be regarded as a system of normative propositions—as a system, in other words, of ought-statements. In such propositions, the mood is imperative rather than indicative. This applies even to plans that merely describe the rewards (e.g., payments) which will attend the performance of specified activities; the obvious intent in such plans is not to describe behavior as it is but rather as it is expected to be. Yet normative statements also have an existential aspect; their realization requires some compliance with the lawfulness of the real world. Hence, insofar as human attitudes have any kind of lawfulness, there is an existential aspect which presents itself to every plan that involves human beings. The fact of such lawfulness in the attitudes of resource users has been supported, we submit, by the findings of the present study.

Lawfulness, of course, expresses the invariance properties of a structural whole. In our study of resource processes we have defined two different kinds of wholes, one of which possesses a determinate structure, the other of which lacks a determinate structure. The former we have called a resource complex, representing it by the symbol X'; the latter we have called a resource congeries, representing it by the symbol X''. In a resource complex all the processes which are observed by the members of a population lie within the set L of practices that are likely in one anothers' behavior; in a resource congeries some of the processes which are observed by at least some members of a population lie outside this set L. The difference can be put in another way: all of the processes in a resource complex are perceived by its participants as being gainful-for-others; some of the processes in a resource congeries are perceived by its participants as being not-gainful-for-others. In this formulation we touch upon the attribute which imparts to a resource complex its structural character and which, therefore, endows it with whatever invariance properties it possesses.

The attribute in question is the attitude of willing conformity on the part of resource users to a system of resource practices; it is the sense of obligation on their part toward particular resource practices as distinct from others. A resource complex is simply the totality of all practices n of which resource users assert $On, -n$. As such, it involves psychologically disruptive mechanisms like ambivalence and repression, and economically inefficient fixities in factor combinations. But it also yields what the economist Commons once described as the "security of expectations"[1] which is prerequisite to every viable social order and, therefore, to every viable resource system.

A resource congeries, on the other hand, is based on the calculating opportunism of its human agents. It is an efficient, amorphous, ever changing aggregate of processes n of which resource users may only assert $-On, -n$. As such, it affords a maximum of formal rationality for its participants. But it also ". . . creates, by rationalising the human mind, a mentality and a style of life incompatible with its own fundamental conditions, motives and social institutions, . . ." (if we may transpose Schumpeter's famous dictum about capitalism to our more general concept of resource congeries).[2] Accordingly, a resource congeries is not a viable type of system.

The structural character of a resource complex, as distinct from a resource congeries, can be further elucidated by reference to three minimum conditions which, in the analysis of Rescher and Oppenheim, every structural whole must meet.[3] These three conditions, and their empirical counterparts in a resource complex, are as follows:

(i) "The whole must possess some *attribute* in virtue of its status as a whole—an attribute peculiar to it and characteristic of it as a whole.

(i) A resource complex possesses *the attribute of willing conformity,* a property compounded out of the sense of obligation which attaches to the discrete resource practices comprising the elements of the complex.

(ii) "The parts of the whole must stand in some special and characteristic *relation* of dependence with one another; they must satisfy some special condition in virtue of their status as parts of a whole.

(ii) The practices of a resource complex, viewed in terms of the attitudinal attributes of idealization, likelihood, comparability relative to value, and obligation, stand in the characteristic *relation of dependence specified in equation 1 of Chapter IX.*

(iii) "The whole must possess some kind of *structure,* in virtue of which certain specifically structural characteristics pertain to it." [4]

(iii) A resource complex possesses *the structure of a lattice,* in virtue of which the characteristics of viability pertain to it.

A resource complex, then, is an entity whose component parts exhibit some lawfulness. The human agents who engage in its practices experience their resource complex as a necessity, but as a necessity to which they willingly accede. Relative to this structural whole, now, a resource plan is a capricious thing, possessing no lawfulness and imposing upon its subjects only an external necessity. In Kantian terms, the norms of a resource complex are autonomous: the subject gives them to himself; but the norms of a resource plan are heteronomous: an outside will imposes them upon the subject. How can the two sets of norms be brought into rapport? Under what conditions will plannees accord a judgment of moral necessity to the normative propositions comprising a plan? More specifically, what is the composition of attitudes which a resource planner needs to count upon if he is to win the consent of resource users to his program? In the words of the sociologist Whetten, "How can the immediate interests of individual owners of renewable natural resources be identified with the interests of society and future generations?" [5]

We may approach this question by regarding a resource plan as part of a culture, in the sense of having at least a conceptual status in people's minds. In this perspective, if the processes which are proposed by the normative propositions of a plan lie outside the set A of adoptable resource processes, the plan is sure to miscarry. If, however, the proposed processes lie within the set A, they will be subject to the same selectivity, and the same sifting and sorting, that any newly available processes undergo. Carrying the analysis a step further, it is possible to differentiate adoptable plans (those whose proposed processes lie within A) according to the magnitude of change which they would require of a resource complex. If this change is beyond some critical magnitude we shall have to assign some of the elements of the plan to the subset γ of C, where γ, as before, denotes the aspect of instability in the set C of socially defined activities. On the other hand, if the change called for by the plan is less than a critical magnitude, we should not assign any elements of the plan to γ. In the first instance, the plan would represent a factor of instability in a people's cultural environment. In the second instance, it would represent a stabilizing factor in the cultural environment.

Now, from what we have already learned it is clear that workable plans of resource *development* are going to call for the first kind of approach; workable plans of resource *conservation* are going to call for the second kind of approach. Success of the former depends on the planner's ability to offer new opportunities for private gain to resource users, to afford them a release of previously inhibited incentives for private gain, and to evoke the calculating opportunism of his subjects. Success of the latter depends on the planner's ability to obscure resource users' perception of private gain, to gratify their incentives for security in personal relationships, and to enlist the willing conformity of his subjects. In the first case, the outcome will be a transition to a resource congeries; in the second case, the outcome will be the maintenance of a resource complex. Equations 2 and 1 (see p. 223), as stated in the preceding chapter, specify the formal conditions necessary for employing these respective approaches to planning. Thus, if a plannee asserts that a newly proposed process is not good or not sure, he will only employ it if it is gainful for himself. On the other hand, if a plannee asserts that a newly proposed resource process is both good and sure, he will feel obliged to employ it if it has the further attribute of being gainful for others as well as for himself.[6]

Plans which do not win the consent of their subjects on either of these counts will become *leges imperfectae,* or else they will succeed only through the bald use of coercive measures. In the latter event, they might achieve a certain validity, but they would not have achieved legitimacy. Moreover, relative to consent, coercion is an expensive method of implementing a plan, and the revenues which it yields have to be weighed against the costs which it entails. Planners generally find it expedient to "économiser les frais de la lutte." [7] Winning plannees' consent, by one of the two routes suggested in equations 1 and 2, is one means of achieving economy in a planning program. In either of these ways a rapport can be reached between the norms of a resource system and the norms of a resource plan. Heteronomous norms can become autonomous norms, with plannees according a legitimacy to the normative propositions comprising a given plan.

These formal considerations take on a practical aspect when we turn to a problem which confronts nearly every government today—that of changing people's resource practices in accordance with some larger national policy objective. There is an imperative need for planners to have an intellectually respectable rationale for what they are doing. Where can they find it? Is it available in the ecological approach to natural resources, which would offer as the only criterion of rational resource planning that of permanence, or long run possibility in a system of resource processes, and which in turn would entail establishing some sort of climax state among organic and physical processes? Is it available in an ethnological approach, according to which the relevant criterion for rational resource planning is the adoptability of one or another system of processes which is, in the limiting case, predicated on the consistency of those processes with important themes in a people's culture? Or is it available in an economic approach, which would define efficiency as the desideratum of rational resource planning and which would entail equating marginal factor costs with marginal net revenue productivities?

We submit that no one of these approaches can, by itself, provide an adequate rationale for what resource planners are doing or are able to do. There is something heroic but futile in the ecological criterion of permanence; there is something aesthetic but anachronistic in the ethnological criterion of adoptability; and there is something rational but precarious in the economic criterion of efficiency. On the other hand, the criterion of plannees' consent is both realistic and progressive. It derives from a systematic theory of resource behavior which is at once adequate to the facts about man as a resource using creature, and adequate as well to the canon of logical consistency with some plausible postulates concerning human behavior generally. These virtues should recommend it to the planner and policy maker who seeks a theory that will give intellectual respectability to his endeavors.

No theory, of course, can be expected to explain all aspects of the realm of events with which it is concerned. Neither can any one theory serve as an all-purpose guide to policy formation. The resource planner needs more than a theory of how resource users *actually* behave; he needs some "as if" theories, some fictional theories, as it were, of how people ought to behave if certain abstract limiting conditions are to be *approached* (even though they can never be reached). Such theories provide the planner with some generalized reference points against which he can plot the relative position which a given resource system occupies on such dimensions as permanence (possibility in the long run), consistency, and efficiency. The theories of ecology, ethnology, and economics offer just such reference points. The three corresponding optima which are defined by these theories, though they can never be simultaneously achieved in real life, nevertheless serve as ideal standards from which a resource system departs at the cost of predictable consequences. The wise planner will use them as canons of what ought to be but can never be. He will turn to a more realistic theory to discover what *can* be. For in his own practical way he knows that man is both a destroyer and a creator of natural resources and is unlikely to ever be otherwise.

NOTES

1. John R. Commons, *Institutional Economics* (New York: Macmillan Co., 1934), p. 705.

2. Joseph Schumpeter, "The Instability of Capitalism," *The Economic Journal*, XXXVIII (1928), 386.

3. Nicholas Rescher and Paul Oppenheim, "Logical Analysis of Gestalt Concepts," *British Journal for the Philosophy of Science*, VI (1955), 89-106.

4. *Ibid.*, p. 90.

5. Nathan L. Whetten, "Sociology and the Conservation of Renewable Natural Resources," *Proceedings of the Inter-American Conference on Conservation of Renewable Natural Resources*, Denver, September 7-20, 1948 (Washington, D. C.: Department of State, Publication 3382), p. 312.

6. If, of course, the plannee perceives the proposed resource process as being gainful only for himself, but as good and sure too, he will also employ the process. But in this case the plan becomes a wholly redundant thing, an epiphenomenon to events as they would have transpired anyway.

7. François Perroux, "Les macrodécisions," *Économie appliquée*, II (1949), 328. This paper presents an interesting analysis of some socioeconomic limits to coercion.

INDEX

Activity, 27f., 31, 45, 101, 124, 136, 145, 151

Adoptability, 28ff., 37, 41, 53, 56f., 77, 82-83, 99ff., 112, 136-37, 154f., 168, 209-10, 248ff.

Africa. *See* Tiv, Bemba

Agents, human, 15, 24ff., 31-33, 74-75, 82f., 89-93, 98ff., 111ff., 181, 194-200, 227ff., 246ff.

Allan, William, 58, 78n, 79n, 80n

Altruism, 229-32, 235-38. *See also* Conformity, Conscience, Consent, Likelihood, Obligation

Ambient, 27-28. *See also* Habitat

Ambivalence, 82ff., 92f., 106, 111-13, 120-24, 128f., 196, 229-31, 235-37, 246

Anderson, Alan Ross, 241n

Aristotle, 19, 37n

Arrow, Kenneth J., 240n, 241n

Bailey, Wilfrid C., 162n, 203n

Baker, Riley E., 163n, 164n, 203n

Barnes, J. R., 162n, 163n, 164n

Barton, Allen H., 109n, 203n, 204n

Batwell, B. L., 17n

Bemba, 60-76

Benedict, Ruth, 38n

Berelson, Bernard, 239n

Beresford, Maurice, 132n, 133n

Bergson, Henri, 210, 230, 239n, 241n

Bertrand, Alvin L., 162n

Biotic community, 21, 24

Birkhoff, Garrett, 204n

Bohannan, Laura, 42, 45, 53n, 54n

Bohannan, Paul, 42, 45, 47, 53n, 54n

Bonnen, C. A., 162n, 163n, 203n

Boulding, Kenneth E., 38n, 78n

Bradley, Harriett, 131n, 133n

Briggs, G. W. G., 54n

Broadhurst, W. L., 162n, 164n, 204n

Brotherton, Charles Benjamin, 164n, 205n

Buchanan, K. M., 54n

Cain, Leonard D., Jr., 205n

Capital, resources as, 13, 136-37, 151, 169, 233

Champion husbandry, 84-98, 113-25

Change, 112-30. *See also* Development, Exogenous factors, Planning

Charlton, J. L., 162n

Cicero, 109n

Ciriacy-Wantrup, S. V., 131n, 161n, 233, 238n, 241n

Citemene, 58-80, 112

Clapham, Sir John, 107n, 108n, 131n, 132n

Climax, 24f., 40, 44-45, 52, 85, 250

Clothier, J. N., 58, 78n, 79n

Coercion, 250

Cohen, Albert K., 38n

Cohen, Morris R., 130n, 239n

Commons, John R., 246, 252n

Comparability, 212-14, 221-35, 241n, 247. *See also* Lattice, Partially ordered system

Complex, resource, 13, 15, 19ff., 28ff., 45, 53, 56-58, 65, 67ff., 74-78, 82-84, 89, 93, 98, 100-6, 112ff., 118-24, 129-30, 168, 172, 197f., 202, 209, 236, 245ff.; defined, 14. *See also* Congeries, resource

Conatus, 208, 236

Conformity, 78, 82, 89ff., 96ff., 103, 106, 111-12, 115ff., 129f., 173-74, 192, 195-97, 209, 230, 235-38, 246ff. *See also* Altruism, Conscience, Consent, Likelihood, Obligation

Congeries, resource, 84, 100, 120, 123-24, 126ff., 168ff., 197ff., 209, 236, 245ff.; defined, 14. *See also* Complex, resource

Conscience, 92, 209f., 229ff., 236ff. *See also* Altruism, Conformity, Consent, Likelihood, Obligation

Consent, 243-51. *See also* Altruism, Conformity, Conscience, Likelihood, Obligation

Conservation, 26, 45, 135-37, 142, 183-88, 207-38, 241n, 244, 249. *See also* Depletion, Planning

Consistency, cultural, 30f., 40, 45-48, 52, 104, 250-51

Content assessment, 211-23

Coombs, Clyde H., 204n

Court, W. H. B., 133n

Cross-cultural design, 16, 136
Culture, 20f., 27, 30f., 67, 100ff., 136,
145-51, 154, 159, 200-3, 248, 251

Demesne. *See* Manor
Depletion of resources, 13, 44, 59, 62,
71, 74, 113, 137, 182-83, 220. *See also*
Conservation, Development, Planning
Development, 135-60, 200-3, 207, 243-44,
249. *See also* Depletion, Exogenous
factors, Planning
Difference, method of, 212-25
Durkheim, Émile, 231, 240n, 241n
Duties. *See* Conscience
Dynamics. *See* Change, Development,
Exogenous factors, Planning

Ecology, 20-26, 37, 40, 44-45, 50-52, 100,
250-52
Economics, 20, 31-35, 37, 40, 48-52, 235,
251-52. *See also* Capital, resources as;
Efficiency; Gainfulness
Ecosystem, 21
Education, 187-88, 220
Efficiency, 32ff., 41, 57-58, 63ff., 82-83,
91, 93-96, 98, 100, 102, 107, 112, 115,
119f., 125f., 129, 166, 195, 230, 236,
246, 251. *See also* Gainfulness
Ellis, W. C., 162n, 163n, 164n
England. *See* Midlands, English
Equilibrium, 21ff., 41, 44
Ernle, Lord, 108n, 127, 131n, 132n,
133n
Ethnology, 20, 26-31, 37, 40, 45-48,
50-52, 101, 250-52
Europe. *See* Midlands, English
Evans, E. Estyn, 107n
Event, 13, 136
Exogenous factors, 84-85, 90, 113, 129,
151-54, 166, 200-3, 208, 236-37

Firey, Walter, 238n
Forde, Daryll, 79n
Frey, John C., 239n
Furon, Raymond, 26, 38n

Gainfulness, 31ff., 50ff., 65, 68, 75-76,
82-85, 90-98, 100-7, 111ff., 166-81,
192-202, 208ff., 220-36, 241n, 245ff.
See also Efficiency
George, W. O., 162n

Gibbs, Marion, 132n
Gonner, E. C. K., 131n, 132n, 133n
Gould, J. D., 133n
Gourou, Pierre, 54n, 78n
Gras, Norman Scott Brien, 133n, 161n
Graves, Bennie Dwane, 205n
Gray, Howard Levi, 107n, 131n, 133n
Green, Thomas Hill, 241n
Groundwater, 139, 143f., 155-60, 169-75,
182-92, 211-24, 237-38

Habitat, 13, 20ff., 66, 100, 137, 143-48,
154, 200-3,
Hailey, Lord, 79n, 80n
Haley, J. Evetts, 163n
Harrington, Edwin Lincoln, 163n
Hasbach, W., 132n, 133n
Hicks, J. R., 236
High Plains. *See* South Plains
Hobhouse, L. T., 241n
Hoglund, C. R., 239n
Homans, George Caspar, 107n, 108n,
131n
Hughes, William F., 162n, 203n, 204n,
205n

Idealization, 212-13, 216-32, 237, 239n,
241n, 247
Incentives, 82-85, 89ff., 102, 106, 111ff.,
119, 130, 166, 173, 181, 185, 189ff.,
201, 229, 236, 249
Incomparability. *See* Comparability
Industrialization, 70ff., 76, 114, 145-48.
See also Technology
Irrigation, 138-42, 157-60, 169-75, 181-
92, 211-24, 237-38

Jacks, G. V., 78n, 107n
Jellinek, Georg, 93, 108n
Johnson, H. M., 204n
Johnson, Willard D., 162n, 163n
Jones, D. L., 162n
Jonson, Ben, 81

Kempski, Jürgen von, 204n
Kendall, Patricia L., 240n
Kluckhohn, Clyde, 38n, 132n, 204n
Kosminsky, E. A., 108n, 131n, 132n

Lang, J. W., 162n
Lasswell, Harold D., 109n, 203n

Lattice, 179-81, 192-200, 204n, 209-11, 212, 225-28, 247. *See also* Comparability, Partially ordered system
Lazarsfeld, Paul F., 109n, 203n, 204n, 240n
Leggat, E. R., 162n
Lerner, Daniel, 109n, 203n
Likelihood, 90ff., 103-7, 111ff., 119ff., 166-81, 192-202, 208ff., 217-36, 245ff. *See also* Altruism, Conformity, Conscience, Consent, Obligation
Lipson, E., 108n, 132n

McArthur, W. C., 203n
Magee, A. C., 162n, 163n, 203n, 204n
Malin, James C., 163n
Manor, 97, 116-22, 125
Market economy, 35, 50ff., 114-22, 125ff., 139, 149-50, 157ff., 234f.
Mead, George H., 206n
Menger, Karl, 240n, 241n
Meredith, H. O., 132n
Merton, Robert K., 132n, 133n, 239n
Midlands, English, 84-98, 113-29
Mill, John Stuart, 212
Minimax, 197
Moe, Edward O., 239n
Molière, 15
Moore, Omar Khayyam, 241n
Morgenstern, Oskar, 206n, 240n
Motheral, Joe R., 162n
Motivation. *See* Incentives
Myrdal, Gunnar, 204n

Nagel, Ernest, 239n
Natural resources, definition of, 13, 136, 151, 154, 160. *See also* Complex, resource; Congeries, resource; Process, resource
Neilson, Nellie, 108n, 132n
Neumann, John von, 206n, 240n
North America. *See* South Plains

Obligation, 212f., 216-38, 240n, 246f. *See also* Altruism, Conformity, Conscience, Likelihood
Odum, Eugene P., 37n
Open field complex, 84, 90-98, 113-25
Opler, Morris Edward, 38n
Oppenheim, Paul, 17n, 131n, 204n, 247, 252n

Opportunism, 120, 124, 129, 139, 200-1, 233, 246, 249
Organic character of resource use. *See* Resource use, structural character of
Orwin, C. S., 107n, 108n

Parain, Charles, 108n, 131n
Parsons, Talcott, 38n, 108n, 132n, 163n, 203n, 206n, 241n
Partially ordered system, 178-81, 192-200, 233. *See also* Comparability, Lattice
Pedersen, Harald A., 162n
Peirce, Charles S., 130n
Perroux, François, 252n
Peters, D. U., 58, 78n, 79n, 80n
Phillips, Frances, 161n, 162n, 164n
Piaget, Jean, 204n
Pirenne, Henri, 131n
Planning, 11-12, 15, 19, 25, 29, 31, 34ff., 50ff., 111, 135, 165-66, 207-8, 220-23, 243ff. *See also* Change, Conservation, Depletion, Development
Plato, 19, 237
Politics, 114-15, 122, 126, 129, 139, 150, 183-91, 217-20, 237-38
Pope, Alexander, 165, 203n
Popper, Karl, 203n, 239n, 240n
Power, Eileen, 108n, 131n, 132n
Practice, resource, 23, 31ff., 42, 89, 93-95, 103, 111, 120, 189, 209f., 246; defined, 14. *See also* Process, resource
Process, resource, 15, 19ff., 56-58, 74, 100-1, 122f., 136-37, 151ff., 168-81, 193-202, 208-10, 246; defined, 13. *See also* Practice, resource
Pugh, J. C., 54n

Ratliff, Ernest C., 161n, 164n, 204n
Regulation, 183-92, 220. *See also* Conformity
Rescher, Nicholas, 17n, 131n, 204n, 247, 252n
Resource, natural. *See* Natural resources; Complex, resource; Congeries, resource
Resource, use, improving. *See* Planning
Resource use, structural character of, 12-15, 19, 36, 69ff., 112, 124, 245-47. *See also* Complex, resource; Congeries, resource
Resource user. *See* Agents, human

Richards, Audrey I., 58, 78n, 79n, 80n
Riches, Naomi, 133n
Rights. *See* Gainfulness
Rodberg, L. S., 11, 16n
Rosenberg, Morris, 109n, 203n, 240n
Ross, Edward Alsworth, 111, 130n
Russell, E. S., 238n

Samuelson, Paul A., 38n
Sanctions, 89, 119, 123, 127, 130, 196ff.
Sauer, Carl O., 37n
Scalapino, R. A., 162n
Scarcity, 20, 31, 136, 209
Schlippe, Pierre de, 17n
Schultz, Theodore W., 163n
Schumpeter, Joseph, 246, 252n
Schwind, Martin, 39, 53n
Scott, Anthony, 161n, 238n
Sears, Paul B., 55, 78n
Security. *See* Likelihood
Seebohm, M. E., 108n, 131n, 132n, 133n
Selection, 19-20, 112, 248
Self interest, 92, 112, 121, 235ff., 248.
    See also Gainfulness, Incentives
Shils, Edward A., 38n, 108n, 132n, 203n, 206n
Sjoberg, Gideon, 17n, 205n
Skrabanek, R. L., 162n
Smith, H. P., 162n
Smith, Robert Trow-. *See* Trow-Smith, Robert
Soil, 44-45, 59-60, 74, 85-86, 113, 127, 144
Solidarity, 191
Sorokin, Pitirim A., 17n, 108n, 132n, 163n, 191, 205n, 239n, 241n
South Plains, 138-51, 155-60, 169-75, 181-92, 211-24, 237-38
Spinoza, 208
Spoehr, Alexander, 27, 38n
Stamp, L. Dudley, 54n, 108n
Street, James H., 162n
Structure of resource use. *See* Complex, resource; Congeries, resource; Resource use, structural character of
Succession, 59, 62ff., 76, 121ff., 139-41
Sweezy, Paul M., 131n
System, resource. *See* Complex, resource; Congeries, resource

Tabor, Leon R., 162n
Tansley, A. G., 25, 37n, 107n

Tarver, James D., 162n
Tawney, R. H., 98, 108n, 131n, 132n, 133n
Technology, 86-87, 91, 94-95, 139, 140-41, 145-48, 157-59
Theme, 27, 30f., 41, 45ff., 251. *See also* Culture
Thibodeaux, B. H., 162n, 163n
Thomas, William L., Jr., 37n, 38n, 78n, 107n
Tiv, 41-54
Trade. *See* Market economy
Trapnell, C. G., 58, 78n, 79n
Trow-Smith, Robert, 107n, 133n, 161n

Uexküll, J. J. von, 26
Use of natural resources, 165-203, 208-9
Utility. *See* Gainfulness

Value, 28, 30, 33, 35, 41, 75, 123, 137, 175-81, 191-200, 209-10, 221-29, 233f., 247. *See also* Comparability, Gainfulness, Likelihood
Viability, 57, 74-75, 78, 98, 113, 121f., 129, 208-9, 231-32, 235, 246f.
Vinogradoff, P., 107n, 108n, 131n, 132n

Wantrup, S. V. Ciracy-. *See* Ciracy-Wantrup, S. V.
Water. *See* Groundwater
Webb, Walter Prescott, 161n, 163n
Weber, Max, 131n, 133n
Weisskopf, V. F., 11, 16n
Whaley, W. Gordon, 162n
Whetten, Nathan L., 248, 252n
Whitaker, J. R., 16n
White, W. N., 162n
Whitehead, Alfred North, 207, 238n
Whiteley, Wilfred, 58, 78n, 79n, 80n
Whittlesey, Derwent, 135, 161n
Whyte, R. O., 78n, 107n
Williams, James Peter, Jr., 205n
Williams, Robin M., Jr., 38n
Wilson, Godfrey, 80n
Wolf, Katherine M., 240n
Woodruff, Edward, P. Jr., 205n

Xenocrates, 106, 109n

Zimmermann, Erich W., 27, 38n, 161n, 162n, 163n, 164n, 238n, 241n

DATE			
DEC 1 4 1982			
NOV 0 5 1996			